D1532402

Faith and the
Studies in Christian Eschatology

Raymond E. Brown, S.S.
Walter Kasper
Gerald O'Collins, S.J.

Edited by
John P. Galvin

PAULIST PRESS
New York and Mahwah, N.J.

236
GaF

Library of Congress Cataloging-in-Publication Data

Faith and the future: studies in Christian eschatology/Raymond E. Brown, Walter Kasper, Gerald O'Collins; edited by John P. Galvin.
    p. cm.
Lectures delivered in Oct. 1992 to celebrate the inauguration of a visiting professorship at the Pontifical College Josephinum, Columbus, Ohio.
Includes bibliographical references.
Contents: Individual salvation and eschatological consummation / Walter Kasper—In the end, love / Gerald O'Collins—Eschatological events accompanying the death of Jesus... / Raymond E. Brown.
    ISBN 0-8091-3455-1 (pbk.)
    1. Eschatology—History of doctrines. I. Brown, Raymond Edward. II. Kasper, Walter. III. O'Collins, Gerald. IV. Galvin, John P.,   1944-
BT823.F35   1994
236—dc20   93-32807
                                                   CIP

Published by Paulist Press
997 Macarthur Boulevard
Mahwah, NJ 07430

Printed and bound in the
United States of America

Contents

Dedicated to
PIO CARDINAL LAGHI
Prefect of the Congregation for Catholic Education

in commemoration of the inauguration of the
Pio Cardinal Laghi Chair
for Visiting Professors in Scripture and Theology
at the Pontifical College Josephinum
Columbus, Ohio
October 20-21, 1992

Preface

The lectures contained in this volume were delivered in October 1992 as part of the celebration to inaugurate an academic chair for visiting professors at the Pontifical College Josephinum in honor of Pio Cardinal Laghi, Prefect of the Congregation for Catholic Education. Upon his departure from the United States as the Apostolic Pro-Nuncio and Chancellor of the Josephinum, a committee of cardinals and bishops promoted the funding of this chair as a means of recognizing his service to the church in this country.

The choice of the eschatological theme uniting these papers was intentional. The organizers of the inaugural events saw this occasion as an opportunity to have three world-renowned scholars present a Catholic perspective on a topic that expectedly will occupy the attention of believers as we approach the beginning of a new millennium.

The Pontifical College Josephinum is grateful to the committee of American cardinals and presidents of the United States Bishops' Conference, chaired by Joseph Cardinal Bernardin, for promoting this academic chair for visiting professors. While the inaugural lectures and this publication are a tribute to Cardinal Laghi, they also reflect the committee's commitment to Catholic scholarship and to the enhancement of seminary formation.

Blase J. Cupich
Pontifical College Josephinum
Columbus, Ohio

Introduction

O ver the course of the twentieth century, eschatology—the study of the "last things"—has moved from the periphery of theological discourse to the heart of theological interest. Growing awareness of the prominence of eschatology in the New Testament—from Jesus' proclamation that "the kingdom of God is at hand" (Mk 1:15) through Paul's expectation of "the day of the Lord [which] will come like a thief in the night" (1 Thess 5:2) to the apocalyptic vision of a "new heaven and a new earth" (Rev 21:1)—has gradually, though in fits and starts, contributed to enhanced attention to eschatological questions on the part of systematic theologians and led to explicit incorporation of eschatological themes and perspectives into reflection on other aspects of systematic theology.

It was therefore highly appropriate for the organizers of the symposium which marked the inauguration of the Pio Cardinal Laghi Chair for Visiting Professors of Scripture and Theology at the Pontifical College Josephinum to choose eschatology as the focal point for the lectures commemorating the chair's institution. The three lectures delivered at the symposium, now slightly revised for publication in this volume, reflect the close relationship and mutual dependence of biblical and systematic theology. It would have been difficult to find a different theme more suited to instituting a professorship which encompasses both biblical and dogmatic specializations.

3

In the first essay, Walter Kasper, Bishop of Rottenburg-Stuttgart and former Ordinary Professor of Dogmatic Theology at the University of Tübingen, surveys the development of eschatological thought in twentieth century Protestant and Catholic theology. Because theological orientations explicit in eschatology permeate the whole of an author's thinking, Kasper's account may also serve as a useful introduction to the history of modern theology and to the overall theological conceptions of several major contemporary theologians.

In the second paper, Gerald O'Collins, S.J., Professor of Fundamental Theology at the Pontifical Gregorian University in Rome, explores possibilities which might lie in reorientation of eschatological thought toward more explicit accentuation of the theme of love. Taking his cue from Dante's evocation of "the love which moves the sun and the other stars," O'Collins uncovers eight characteristics of love which enable it to perform an integrating role in eschatology—as it does in Christian life.

In the final contribution, Raymond E. Brown, S.S., Auburn Distinguished Professor Emeritus of Biblical Studies at Union Theological Seminary in New York, studies in detail the eschatological phenomena associated in the gospels with Jesus' crucifixion. Special attention is devoted to the raising of the holy ones, as noted in Matthew 27:51-53. Brown's detailed exegesis of these brief but complex biblical passages provides an example of the methodical procedure and balanced judgment needed in the interpretation of all eschatological assertions and apocalyptic imagery.

While the papers incorporated in this volume do not constitute a comprehensive eschatology, they afford an initial overview of some central eschatological themes and shed light on the complexities of reflection in an area of theology and biblical scholarship which has been both oft neglected and much abused. Each in its own way contributes to the re-examination of eschatological themes incumbent on contemporary theology.

For assistance in editing these papers for publication I am grateful to Mr. Christopher J. Malloy.

John P. Galvin
The Catholic University of America
Washington, D.C.

Individual Salvation and Eschatological Consummation

WALTER KASPER

I. A Testimony to Our Hope—A Test of Our Faith

"The bureau of eschatology is generally closed these days."[1] With this comment Ernst Troeltsch characterized the state of modern theology at the beginning of the twentieth century. In the 1970s an updated version of this dictum, formulated some years earlier by Hans Urs von Balthasar, made the rounds. Von Balthasar felt that the eschatological bureau was now, so to speak, "working overtime."[2] Indeed, the subject of hope in theology has been acquiring new topicality in recent years.

The present eschatological "boom" is a "sign of the times." It is an expression of the crisis of the basic principle of modern times: freedom. At the beginning of the modern age, human beings gained a completely new understanding of what freedom meant. They discovered that they were not completely at the mercy of remote natural forces or supposedly immutable political institutions, but were rather the architects of their own fate. Modern science and technology provided them with the means of shaping their own future. This led to a situation whereby humanity has witnessed far more changes in the last two hundred years than in the space of the whole two thousand years

that had gone before. The hallmark of the eighteenth and nineteenth centuries was thus a strong belief in progress. But to the
same degree that belief in progress grew, the subject of eschatology seemed to become more and more obsolete.

However, belief in progress suffered a series of considerable blows as early as the beginning of this century, the first
being World War I. It was during the post-war period that
Oswald Spengler wrote the widely read book *The Decline of the
West*.[3] Existential philosophy, which developed at much the
same time, attempted to reflect on the widespread uncertainty
and fear engendered by these events. The Second World War
provided even more forceful evidence of the ambiguous nature
of technological progress and its proneness to abuse. However, it
was the global ecological problems that have emerged over the
last decades which have finally succeeded in fully exposing the
"limits of growth."[4] The flipside of technological progress has
also become more than apparent in the strain on and destruction
of the environment that we are witnessing. We have seen not
only the collapse of evolutionary belief in progress, but also that
of revolutionary belief in progress, as the demise of Marxist
communism in central and eastern Europe demonstrates only too
clearly. As a result, for many people today, belief in progress has
been transformed into a dread of what is yet to come.

The lack of perspective caused in the human spirit by the
loss of faith in the ideology of progress has created a spiritual
vacuum and along with many other causes has paved the way
for radical ideologies and enthusiastic utopias, the violent effects
of which are being sorely felt at the present time. The crisis can
be said to consist of a number of factors: a catastrophic feeling
of meaninglessness, an erosion of fundamental values and a
complete lack of basic consensus. Furthermore, there is an
absence of far-reaching goals capable of inspiring enthusiasm,
commitment and a willingness to make sacrifices. A crisis of the
human spirit of this magnitude must ultimately have fatal consequences. For hope is not a commodity that people either have or

do not have; hope is of the very essence of human existence. When there is no hope for the future, life becomes completely meaningless. The question of the future is thus both the focus and the paradigm of the question of human salvation.

The current situation presents a particular challenge to Christians. They are required to bear public witness to the hope that is in them (cf. 1 Pet 3:15). In the face of the questions, fears, conflicts and hopes of the world in which we live, they must ensure that they are a living witness to the potential for hope that is central to Christian belief. We must therefore deal with the following questions: How can we express biblical and ecclesiastical eschatology in contemporary terms? How can we convey the essence of eschatology in language which succeeds in formulating comprehensible and helpful answers to the pressing questions of our times? The challenge which Christians face is thus also a challenge to theology.

II. The Problem of Communicating Theological Concepts

The theology of the twentieth century began with the rediscovery of the future as the fundamental dimension of Christian faith. This rediscovery is inextricably linked to the names of Franz Overbeck, Johannes Weiss and Albert Schweitzer.[5] It is undoubtedly linked to the crisis of the then prevalent form of optimistic cultural Christianity espoused by the middle classes, a crisis which became apparent after the First World War. Until this point in time, the theological doctrine of the afterlife was no more than a rather insignificant and harmless tract on "the last things." It then developed an all-embracing perspective. Eschatology became the storm-center of theology. At the time, Karl Barth said: "A Christianity which is not absolutely and completely eschatology has absolutely and completely nothing to do with Christ."[6] Karl Rahner thus rightly designated Christianity as the religion of the absolute future.[7] And Joseph Ratzinger has demonstrated on a number of occasions that the

rediscovery of the central significance of eschatology has served
to reopen the debate as to what the core of Christianity is.[8]

Through this process of universalization, the term "eschatology" has, however, often been overstretched. It is used in contemporary theology to cover all manner of things in a wide vari-
ety of contexts. The rediscovery of biblical eschatology therefore also opened wide the doors to widespread ideological abuse
of the theological perspective of the future. Eschatology formed
a series of alliances with the successive intellectual trends that
were fashionable for a time.

Theology seems to have repeatedly dressed itself in bor-
rowed robes. This naturally raises the question as to what the
unique and unadulterated essence of the Christian hope for the
future is. Not that one could ever hope to isolate the Christian
proprium as one would a chemically pure element; it can only be
expressed in human and therefore also in historically condi-
tioned terms. There is no such thing as timeless theology. But
theology must make discerning and creative use of the intellectual possibilities of an age and translate the Christian faith into a
language that people can understand, and it must also address
the questions of the time. This task must be accomplished in
such a way that no tame and assimilated form of Christianity
results, but that rather the challenge inherent in Christianity is
brought to bear on the given situation.

This brings us to a difficult fundamental problem in contemporary eschatology: that of using modern thought patterns to
communicate the message of traditional Judeo-Christian eschatology, which is couched in apocalyptical categories. Indeed
from the moment Albert Schweitzer rediscovered it, eschatology
has been struggling with this very problem. It found expression
in the following questions: Do the apocalyptic ideas we find in
the Bible mean anything at all to twentieth century people? Are
they not part and parcel of a worldview which has finally
become obsolete? Are apocalyptic models perhaps no more than

time-bound images which are employed in an attempt to describe the completely different reality of biblical eschatology?

Questions of this sort became doubly pressing in the newly found prosperity of the 1950s and 1960s. At the same time, the debate on demythologization that had been launched by Rudolf Bultmann during the war was creating a stir.[9] Trying to combine modern rational thinking with the biblical message, Bultmann attempted an existential interpretation. This was the positive side of his so-called demythologization: objective apocalyptical statements about the absolute future were interpreted as being statements about authentic human existence. However, the consequence of this approach is that the real future in store for human beings is reinterpreted to mean futurity as a human existential. That led to the elimination of the temporal character of eschatology: "In every moment slumbers the possibility of being the eschatological moment. You must awaken it."[10] Imminent expectation of the kingdom of God thus became permanent expectation.

Another attempt at a synthesis between modern and biblical thinking was initiated by Pierre Teilhard de Chardin. Keeping to the framework of modern evolutionist thinking, Teilhard de Chardin tried to interpret Christ as the ultimate aim of the cosmic process of evolution. He understood the Christian hope of Christ's second coming in glory to refer to the concentration and penetration of all reality through Jesus Christ.[11]

It was not until the end of the 1960s and the 1970s that apocalypticism came to be viewed in a positive light again, due to what we call "political theology" and to Jürgen Moltmann's closely related "theology of hope."[12] Something similar is true of the work of Wolfhart Pannenberg.[13] These models have rediscovered the critically liberating potency inherent in the biblical testimony to the resurrection of the dead, the last judgment and the kingdom of God. They have underlined the fact that the kingdom of God has already begun to dawn in the here and now, and that, as Christians, we are called to cooperate in establishing

God's reign. The horizontal dimension, the historically future aspect of Christian hope, was thus again given its due emphasis.

III. The Focus: The Problem of Dual Eschatology

Both existential and political theology, each in its own way, were concerned by and large with the contemporary relevance of central biblical concepts. Meanwhile Catholic dogmatic theology tried to reinterpret the dogmatic contents of eschatological hope itself. Almost the entire body of the dogmatic tradition underwent a process of critical rereading. In doing so, theologians became particularly aware of the problem of the relationship between biblical eschatology with its linear perception of time and more worldly understanding of the end of time on the one hand and Greek transcendental eschatology with its more other-worldly approach on the other. The crucial question which emerged was whether and to what extent the Greek metaphysical view of the personal immortality of the soul was compatible with the biblical expectation of a general resurrection of the body at the end of time. Or to put it another way: What is the relationship between personal eschatology, where the individual is judged after death, and universal eschatology, which involves the second coming of Christ to judge the world? To put it in a nutshell: the central issue became the problem of dual eschatology.

The background to these questions had been dealt with much earlier in Protestant theology by Paul Althaus and Oscar Cullmann.[14] The Catholic theologians Gisbert Greshake and Gerhard Lohfink tried to formulate an original solution. Their answer can be summarized as follows: resurrection in death. In death, the whole human being passes into eternity—a reality beyond time and equally proximate to every age. Thus, parousia and resurrection occur in death. This view seems to conform with the scriptural idea of temporal imminence and also removes the onus of having to retain the concepts of apocalyptic speculation alien to modern thinking. It sees the end of time as constantly occurring all along the line of history.[15]

Among others, Joseph Ratzinger in particular took issue with this position. He vehemently defended the assertions of the Christian tradition, according to which, after death, the human soul enters into an "intermediary state" where it awaits the resurrection of the body at the end of time.[16] A hard-hitting controversy between the dissenting parties ensued and has still not been completely resolved to this day.[17] There are two main points of contention. The first is a problem of terminology. Is it permissible for theology to abandon the traditional terminology of the church? Is it legitimate to interpret the term "resurrection" in a way that is alien to the traditional usage of the term? Is theology not in danger of maneuvering itself into a linguistic and conceptual ghetto by abandoning the term "soul," at the same time making dialogue with other religions more difficult? The second is a theological problem concerning the "intermediary state" between death and resurrection at the end of time. The issue is the relationship between individual and general eschatology. Is the doctrine of an intermediary state a binding article of faith? Or is it to be viewed as merely a replaceable model of thought which has been presupposed by Christian doctrine in the past?[18]

In 1979 the Congregation for the Doctrine of the Faith stated its position on these questions in a declaration entitled "On Certain Questions Concerning Eschatology."[19] It upheld traditional terminology, in particular the term "soul," and excluded all ways of thinking or speaking that would render meaningless or unintelligible the church's prayers, its funeral rites and religious rites for the dead. This declaration emphasizes the distinction between individual eschatology at death and general eschatology at the end of time as a binding article of faith. The doctrine of the intermediary state is not mentioned directly, but is a logical prerequisite for this position. However, this does not mean that the underlying problem of understanding the doctrine properly has been solved. On the contrary, it raises the issue anew. A solution can be found only by means of a detailed and fundamental examination of the very basis and core of Christian hope.

IV. The Way to a Solution: Christological Concentration

The first important step toward a solution to the problem was undertaken by Karl Rahner in his outline of a hermeneutics of eschatological statements.[20] Rahner succeeded in demonstrating that eschatology does not intend to be the speculative account of an eye-witness to a future event. The "Sitz im Leben" of eschatological statements is rather the present experience of the gift of salvation through Jesus Christ. According to Rahner, eschatological statements are simply a transposition of Christology and Christian anthropology into the mode of consummation. Thus Jesus Christ himself is the hermeneutical principle of all eschatological statements. Rahner states: "Anything that cannot be read and understood as a Christological assertion is not a genuine eschatological assertion."[21]

Hans Urs von Balthasar arrived at the same conclusion by a different route. From the biblical point of view, the eschaton is not "a thing," but God himself. When Jesus speaks of the coming of the kingdom of God, he is talking about God's own coming. In the death and resurrection of Jesus, God's coming took place once and for all. The eschaton is thus Jesus Christ. The "last things" are inseparable aspects of the Christological event. This means that for von Balthasar the realized eschatology characteristic of St. John's gospel assumes fundamental significance. Of course, von Balthasar's understanding of realized eschatology is anything but superficial. On the contrary, he succeeds in integrating the horizontal, temporal drama into the vertical drama of God's entering the dimension of time.[22] Thus the linear or horizontal scheme of Jewish eschatology is interrupted by vertical eschatology. In Jesus Christ, ultimate reality becomes present in the provisional reality of history. Unlike the gnostic version of eschatology, this vertical eschatology is rooted in the historical reality of the incarnation. When compared with both Jewish and Greek eschatology, Christian hope proves to be something qualitatively new.

The Christological concentration which is characteristic of the eschatology of Karl Rahner and Hans Urs von Balthasar is also accepted by Joseph Ratzinger, Gisbert Greshake and Gerhard Lohfink. This represents an essential point of convergence in the otherwise so controversial present debate on eschatology. This convergence is all the more significant because in the face of our time's multifarious modern utopias, progressive ideologies and visions for the future, it unanimously insists that Jesus Christ is the unsurpassable, ultimate destiny of humanity, indeed of every individual. He is therefore the ultimate yardstick of history, the judge of the living and the dead.

This point of convergence has consequences for our understanding of the doctrine of the intermediary state. The meaning of the doctrine of the intermediary state and of the distinction between individual and universal eschatology acquires new intelligibility. Individual and universal eschatology are no longer two unconnected concepts but instead become unified in a more comprehensive, elongated form of eschatology. This model does not envision a double judgment. The last judgment is rather a complete revelation of what has taken place in the individual judgment. It determines each individual's ultimate place in the kingdom of God in its consummate form. This explains why the New Testament uses cosmic symbols when talking about the parousia. The parousia both reveals and completes the divine mystery of salvation in Jesus Christ. Parousia means that Jesus Christ is definitively revealed as Lord and recognized as such. The term "second coming" is thus perhaps rather inappropriate and prone to misunderstanding. For it is not a question of repeating something which has already taken place. In reality it is a question of the consummation of Jesus' one and only coming. So, instead of talking about the second coming, it is better to give preference, as does scripture, to the term "parousia" when referring to the ultimate public coming of Jesus Christ in glory.

V. Philosophical and Biblical Considerations

The comprehensive Christological conception which we have been examining thus far has not yet provided an answer to the question of the intermediary state between the death of the individual and the general resurrection at the end of time. However, the foundations necessary for a possible answer have been laid. Insights gained from philosophy and from biblical theology can provide valuable support when attempting to formulate an answer.

One important point of access to the problem in hand is provided by a passage from Origen's seventh homily on the book of Leviticus. Origen says: "You will enter into joy then if you leave this life in holiness. But your full joy will only come when not one of your members is lacking. Wherefore you must wait for others, just as others have waited for you. Surely, too, if you who are a member have not perfect joy as long as a member is missing, how much more will he, our Lord and Savior, consider his joy incomplete while any member of his body is missing....He is loath to receive his perfect happiness without you, that is, without his people who constitute his body and his members."[23]

This text shows that salvation and judgment concern individuals in person. However, the individual is and has its being in relation to others. This means that the individual cannot reach a perfected state until all other human beings have reached that state as well. Individual and general eschatology are therefore essentially interdependent. This train of thought is also fully compatible with the biblical conception of the body. In the Bible, the term "body" does not just mean corporality, but rather embraces each and every aspect of the human being. Nor does the Bible see the human being as a hermetically closed personality. Instead, the individual is woven into the whole fabric and history of the world, including its solidarity and intercommunication. Correspondingly, death, according to the Old Testament, is synonymous with entry into "Sheol." Yet the essence of Sheol is a lack of communication. Seen from this perspective, the resurrection of the dead is a process in which the full communication which has been interrupted by death is restored and in which everything finds its rightful place.

Yet human beings live not only in relation to other human beings, but also in relation to their environment. Having a body, they are part of the environment. Conversely, through the body the world is part of the human being. One can even say that the material world acquires meaning only in the corporality of human beings. This anthropocentric worldview has foundations in the apocalyptic thinking of the Bible. Through the first Adam's decision to be disobedient, the whole cosmos is subjected to transitoriness. Through the obedience of the new Adam, through his death and his exaltation, the whole cosmos is redeemed.[24] Thus, the individual and indeed humanity as a whole cannot reach their consummate form until the whole cosmos has been brought to consummation as well.

But cosmic consummation is more than just the ripe fruit of evolution and history. It is more than the successive harvesting or absorption of time into the dimension of eternity. It must rather be viewed as something new, as a new creative act of God. For only the Creator has unlimited access to and control over natural and cosmic conditions. But there is also another important reason why cosmic consummation must be regarded as a creative act of God. History does not simply mature into a state of perfection; history is rather the scene of the battle which is constantly raging between the kingdom of God and its opponent, the kingdom of evil. Theodicy and anthropodicy require that the conflict between truth and falsehood, justice and injustice be resolved and that absolute justice be established. In a word: there must be an end to all nonsense. It is the fulfillment of this very basic hope that is meant when scripture talks in apocalyptic language about the Lord in the end destroying his adversary, who refuses to acknowledge God's holiness and shows nothing but contempt for human dignity.

The details of how the consummation of the world and of history are to be achieved through the fire of the last judgment remain a mystery to which only God knows the answer. Since God is and remains a mystery, there is no place for foreknowledge or calculations in this matter. Nor can there be any concrete depictions of the final state. All that hope requires is the certitude that the eschatological event is a reality, the knowledge that God is faithful and that God has accepted the world definitively in Jesus Christ. The world and its history are therefore not at the mercy of arbitrary forces. Instead, at the end of time, God will be "all in all" (1 Cor 15:28). Every believer can therefore say with conviction: "Non confundar in aeternum."

VI. A Place in the Communion of Saints

One of the main difficulties, when envisaging individual salvation and eschatological consummation as a differentiated unity, lies in defining the complex relationship between time and eternity. When tackling this question, two approaches must be discounted from the outset, as they prove to be quite incompatible with the Christian faith. These are on the one hand monism, which denies any distinction between time and eternity, and on the other hand dualism, which postulates that time and eternity are completely incongruent. In popular thought patterns we encounter more of an inclination to favor dualistic models than a monistic approach. More involuntarily than by analogy, eternity is commonly conceived of as timelessness, as an abolition, rejection or interruption of time. This leads to the conclusion that Christ's coming in glory is synonymous with the end of the world, or with the end of time. Death is thus thought to be entry into timelessness. But then one is faced with the question as to how eternal life as a timeless phenomenon can be logically compatible with waiting for the "end" of the world.

This is not the place to go into the complex relationship between time and eternity in great detail. But this much may be said: from the Christian point of view, God created the world with time. So time is also a symbol or a parable for God's eternity. The relationship between time and eternity is that of an analogy; in spite of the great similarity between the two, it must be said that the difference between them is even greater. Eternity does not simply abolish time, but it elevates and consummates it. The intermediary state can therefore not be conceived of as being completely timeless, not least because time is a constituent element of the world and of human life.

What consequences does this conclusion have for the state between individual death and cosmic consummation? It means that in it, human beings have two perspectives, one retrospective, looking back on their personal history on earth, and one anticipatory, looking forward to the consummation that lies in store. There is no other way to imagine how we, who are still alive, can enter into any sort of "communion of saints" with the dead, who have already entered eternity. There is no other way of justifying our prayers for the dead or for requesting their intercession for us. Those who are dead still hope and pray in solidarity with us for the ultimate consummation of the world.

It may therefore be said that the world to come does not simply abolish this world, but instead consummates it in a way which surpasses all human understanding. Correspondingly, Jesus' coming in glory does not mean the end, but the consummation of the world, not the end of time, but its fulfillment and completion. Just as the world was not created in time but together with time, so its re-creation will not take place in time but together with time. So we cannot talk about day X as the day of consummation. There will be no last generation, which alone will witness the coming of Christ. The parousia is not about Jesus Christ coming again in the dimension of time. On the cross

and in the exaltation of Jesus, time is embraced and suffused by
the eternal. In the parousia, this process is revealed in glory.

VII. Practical Concretization

The attempt to determine the correct relationship between
individual salvation and eschatological consummation is not an
example of idle theological speculation. The hot debates on the
subject cannot be brushed aside as being no more than petty
bickering among theologians. They are of elemental importance
to the practice of living faith; they bear witness to the hope that
is in us (1 Pet 3:15). In the face of the diverse questions pressing
on modern human beings, we are presented with the challenge
of making the profound truth of living Christian hope comprehensible to people today. As Christians, this challenge presents
itself to us from two angles; we are confronted today on the one
hand with an overwhelming lack of perspective and on the other
hand with a veritable flood of ideologies which are traded and
consumed like any old commodity.

In the light of what has been said thus far, Christian hope
can be summed up as a hope which is lived in solidarity.
Christian hope looks to the realization of true community both
between human beings and God and among human beings themselves. It leads neither to an egotistical concern with personal
salvation, nor to the conclusion that the individual simply dis-
solves into some diffuse cosmic process. Today we can confi-
dently refute both of these errors. The solidarity which is intrin-
sic to Christian hope means that the decision that we make as
individuals for or against Jesus Christ concerns not only ourselves. It is not a question of our personal salvation alone. When
we make this decision it is always done in solidarity with the
rest of the world; it always has repercussions for the salvation of
the world as a whole.

Furthermore, Christian hope is nourished by our faith in
the fact that the absolute future is already a perceptible reality.

The consummation of the world, which Christian faith speaks of in symbolic language, is not a process which has nothing to do with our living and dying in the here and now. The absolute future is as close to us as God is. For the absolute future is God, who gave himself once and for all in Jesus Christ. In Jesus Christ, God has ultimately made life victorious over death, truth victorious over falsehood, and justice and love victorious over hatred and violence. Faith in the victory of life, love and truth is a source of encouragement and strength in our own struggle for life, love and truth. When scripture says that love lasts forever (1 Cor 13:8), this means that the works of love will also last forever,[25] that nothing done in love can ever be lost or be done in vain. Moreover, even those acts of love which remain unacknowledged by others are ultimately and irrevocably rooted in eternal reality.

The church is the sacrament, that is, the sign and instrument, of salvation. The church is thus the sacrament of hope for the world. But do people still perceive the church as a symbol of hope? Does the widespread despair people have about the future of society not apply equally to the future of the church? The church can be the sacrament of hope only if it succeeds in voicing its hope clearly and unequivocally for all to hear, if it avoids succumbing to dread of the future, and if it does not fall victim to a pale and paltry form of popular humanism lacking the decisive salt of Christian faith. The world does not need a duplication of its hope; still less does it need a duplication of its despair.

The church can be a convincing symbol of hope only if it truly lives the beatitudes of the sermon on the mount and if it hopes with and for those who are poor, who mourn, who renounce violence and who hunger and thirst for justice. In short, the church must stand by and stand up for those who, humanly speaking, have no reason left to hope, but who, like Abraham, may still hope against all hope (see Rom 4:18). Thus the option for the poor is essential for the eschatological testimony of the church.

A hope which both manifests solidarity and is universal has nothing to do with human utopias or ideologies. It is rooted in the faith that God is our hope, the eschaton of our lives, indeed of history as a whole, and in the faith that nothing can separate us from the love of Christ (see Rom 8:35). On the contrary, in the end God will be "all in all" (1 Cor 15:28). Looked at this way, eschatology is certainly anything but an insignificant and harmless afterthought tacked on at the end of Christian dogmatics. It is far more than that; indeed it is the perspective of the entirety of Christian faith. Eschatology alone is capable of making faith dynamic and opening up to it unforeseen dimensions. Through eschatology, faith becomes hope for the world.

Notes

1. Ernst Troeltsch, *The Christian Faith: Based on Lectures Delivered at the University of Heidelberg in 1912 and 1913,* ed. Gertrud von le Fort (Minneapolis: Fortress, 1991), p. 38. The German original was published in 1925.

2. Hans Urs von Balthasar, "Some Points of Eschatology," *The Word Made Flesh: Explorations in Theology I* (San Francisco: Ignatius, 1989), p. 255. This essay was originally published in 1957.

3. Oswald Spengler, *The Decline of the West,* 2 vols. (New York: A.A. Knopf, 1926-28).

4. Cf. Dennis L. Meadows, ed., *The Limits to Growth: A Report for the Club of Rome's Project on the Predicament of Mankind,* 2nd ed. (New York: New American Library, 1974).

5. Cf. Franz Overbeck, *Über die Christlichkeit unserer heutigen Theologie* (Leipzig, 1873); Johannes Weiss, *Jesus' Proclamation of the Kingdom of God* (Philadelphia: Fortress, 1971; German original: 1892); Albert Schweitzer, *The Quest of the Historical Jesus: A Critical Study of Its Progress from Reimarus to Wrede* (New York: A. & C. Black, 1910).

6. Karl Barth, *The Epistle to the Romans* (London: Oxford

University Press, 1968), p. 314; revised translation. The German original of this edition was published in 1922.

7. Karl Rahner, "Marxist Utopia and the Christian Future of Man," *Theological Investigations 6* (Baltimore: Helicon, 1969), pp. 59-68.

8. Cf., e.g., Joseph Ratzinger, "Salvation History, Metaphysics and Eschatology," *Principles of Catholic Theology: Building Stones for a Fundamental Theology* (San Francisco: Ignatius, 1987), pp. 171-190, and "Eschatology and Utopia," *Church, Ecumenism and Politics* (New York: Crossroad, 1988), pp. 237-254.

9. Rudolf Bultmann, "New Testament and Mythology," *New Testament and Mythology and Other Basic Writings,* ed. Schubert M. Ogden (Philadelphia: Fortress, 1984), pp. 1-43. Bultmann's essay was originally published in 1941.

10. *History and Eschatology: The Presence of Eternity* (New York: Harper, 1962), p. 155.

11. Cf. *The Divine Milieu* (New York: Harper, 1960).

12. Cf. Johann Baptist Metz, *The Theology of the World* (New York: Herder, 1969), and Jürgen Moltmann, *Theology of Hope: On the Ground and the Implications of a Christian Eschatology* (New York: Harper & Row, 1967).

13. Cf. *Theology and the Kingdom of God* (Philadelphia: Westminster, 1969).

14. Cf. Paul Althaus, *Die letzten Dinge: Lehrbuch der Eschatologie,* 5th ed. (Gütersloh: C. Bertelsmann, 1949), and Oscar Cullmann, *Immortality of the Soul or Resurrection of the Dead?: The Witness of the New Testament* (London: Epworth, 1958).

15. Cf. Gisbert Greshake and Gerhard Lohfink, *Naher-wartung—Auferstehung—Unsterblichkeit,* 5th ed. (Freiburg: Herder, 1986).

16. Cf. Joseph Ratzinger, *Eschatology: Death and Eternal Life* (Washington: Catholic University of America, 1988).

17. In addition to the works already noted, cf. Gisbert

Greshake, "Theologiegeschichtliche und systematische Überlegungen zum Verständnis der Auferstehung," in Gisbert Greshake and Jacob Kremer, *Resurrectio Mortuorum: Zum theologischen Verständnis der leiblichen Auferstehung* (Darmstadt: Wissenschaftliche Buchgesellschaft, 1986), pp. 163-371.

18. The controversy between Greshake and Ratzinger is studied thoroughly in Gerhard Nachtwei, *Dialogische Unsterblichkeit: Eine Untersuchung zu Joseph Ratzingers Eschatologie und Theologie* (Erfurter Theologische Studien 54) (Leipzig: St. Benno, 1986), pp. 70-180.

19. *AAS* 71 (1979): 939-943. For an English translation cf. Austin Flannery, ed., *Vatican Council II: More Postconciliar Documents* (Northport: Costello, 1982), pp. 500-504.

20. "The Hermeneutics of Eschatological Assertions," *Theological Investigations 4* (Baltimore: Helicon, 1966), pp. 323-346.

21. Ibid., p. 343.

22. Cf. "Eschatologie im Umriss," *Pneuma und Institution* (Einsiedeln: Johannes, 1974), pp. 410-455, and *Theodramatik IV: Das Endspiel* (Einsiedeln: Johannes, 1983).

23. Cited according to Henri de Lubac, *Catholicism: A Study of Dogma in Relation to the Corporate Destiny of Mankind* (New York: Mentor-Omega, 1964), p. 239. For the Latin text (the Greek original is not extant) cf. Marcel Borret, ed., *Origène: Homélies sur le Lévitique 1 (Homélies I-VII)* (SC 286) (Paris: Cerf, 1981), pp. 318, 320.

24. Cf. Gen 1–3; Rom 5:12-21; 1 Cor 15:21-23, 45-49.

25. Cf. art. 39 of the Second Vatican Council's Pastoral Constitution on the Church in the Modern World, *Gaudium et spes.*

In the End, Love

GERALD O'COLLINS, S.J.

"God created Adam to have someone upon whom to shower gifts."[1]

In his first encyclical, *Redemptor hominis* of 1979, Pope John Paul II highlighted the way love brings understanding. "Man," he wrote, "cannot live without love. He remains a being that is incomprehensible for himself, his life is senseless, if love is not revealed to him, if he does not encounter love" (n. 10).[2]

Those words could well be adapted and applied to the specific human mystery of death and life after death. As they move toward their end, human beings cannot live without love. As they travel toward their own individual deaths and the consummation of all things, they remain incomprehensible to themselves and their world remains senseless unless that love is revealed which can illuminate their personal end and the end of the universe.

I invite you to join with me in an experiment and look with the eyes of love at the eschaton, our personal eschaton and the eschaton of all things. In other words, could the theme of love prove a useful hermeneutic for exploring individual and general eschatology? Does love help us to understand and interpret a little better the last things? The invitation is to join me in an exercise of *amor quaerens intellectum eschatologicum,* love seeking eschatological understanding.

Can love be pressed into service in that field of Christian doctrine which George Bush has caused to be called "eschatology"? I am referring not to the former president of the United States but to a nineteenth century writer who was professor of Hebrew at New York City University. The *Oxford English Dictionary* credits that George Bush with introducing "eschatology" into the English language through his 1845 book, *Anastasis: or the Doctrine of the Resurrection of the Body, Rationally and Scripturally Considered.*[3]

A seventeenth century German Lutheran theologian named Abraham Calov (1612-1686) is normally recalled as the first to coin the term, at least in Latin, with his book *Eschatologia sacra.*[4] More than a century later Friedrich Schleiermacher (1768-1834) gave his very influential support both to the term and to the field which it named, and "eschatology" entered the common language of theology, at least among Protestants.[5] From German theological language "eschatology" passed into other languages: into English, for example, with George Bush's 1845 book, *Anastasis.*

All power to Abraham Calov, Friedrich Schleiermacher and George Bush. But let us remember a much earlier Christian writer who, without ever using the term "eschatology," wrote much about the last things. He is also the author who gave me the idea that love just might be a good or even the best key to eschatology. I am thinking, of course, of Dante Alighieri (1265-1321). In his *Divine Comedy* Dante went on an imaginary journey through hell and purgatory to paradise, led by the two figures of Virgil and Beatrice. They are normally taken to represent reason and faith, respectively. But whatever one says about Virgil's representative role in the *Divine Comedy*, it seems to me quite implausible not to credit Beatrice with representing love as well as faith. Love allowed Dante to explore imaginatively the last things—right through to the end and his vision of the divine

love which "moves the sun and the other stars." Love let Dante
see with the heart. Perhaps love can allow us to make a kind of
eschatological pilgrimage and see the last things with our heart.
This has not often been done. In fact, has it ever been done? Has
any theologian ever written a fully deployed eschatology in the
key of love?

The manualist theology, familiar to most of us, went
doggedly through all the last things: death, personal judgment,
purgatory, hell, heaven, the general resurrection of the dead, the
second coming, the general judgment and the final consummation of the world. Along the way there could be various excur-
suses and scholia—on such matters as the situation of the sepa-
rated soul and the nature of the risen body (with its agility, sub-
tlety and other qualities). That manualist tradition paid little
attention to love, except for two questions: the suffering of souls
in purgatory and the nature of heavenly bliss.

Right at the end of the manualist tradition, Ludwig Ott in
his *Fundamentals of Catholic Dogma* exemplifies well the scant
attention paid to love in the whole treatment of the last things.
As regards the punishment of souls in purgatory, he tells us that
they long to be intimately united with God and so they suffer.
Then heaven is described as "a place and condition of perfect
supernatural bliss, which consists in the immediate vision of
God and in the perfect love of God associated with it." Here Ott
gives a brief airing to the debate between the Thomists and the
Scotists. Both schools maintained three elements in describing
the situation of the blessed: *visio, amor* and *gaudium* or *fruitio*
(the immediate vision of God with the perfect love and complete
joy which that vision brings). The basic act of heavenly bliss
according to the Thomists is the vision, but according to the
Scotists it is being united with God through love. Apart from
those two specific questions on the nature of purgatorial suffering and heavenly bliss, love makes no other appearance in Ott's
eschatology.[6]

The closing decades of the manualist tradition coincided

with the profound growth and development in twentieth century Catholic theology which fed into the Second Vatican Council. The post-conciliar situation brought its flood-tide of fresh publications and, in particular, new eschatologies. They have come from German authors like Gisbert Greshake, Karl Rahner, and Joseph Ratzinger, from Spanish authors like Juan Luis Ruiz de la Peña, from Italian authors like Marcello Bordoni and Nicola Ciola, and from American authors like Zachary Hayes and others.[7]

As much as any of the post-conciliar works, the 1976 section of *Mysterium Salutis* devoted to eschatology reflects signs of renewal in this and other areas of theology. Biblical, patristic and other historical sources are handled with more precise scholarship than in much of the manualist era. The approach runs genetically and no longer regressively: that is to say, instead of taking as the starting point the latest teaching of the official magisterium on eschatological matters and looking back for supporting arguments, the focus is rather on how the church's theology and teaching developed from the time of the New Testament on. Karl Rahner's seminal essay of 1960, "The Hermeneutics of Eschatological Assertions,"[8] is strongly in evidence, as is that massive trend toward doing all theology in an eschatological key which Karl Barth[9] encouraged in Protestant theology and which climaxed with Jürgen Moltmann's *Theology of Hope.*[10]

Not only ecumenical influences but also philosophical and cultural factors (such as Ernst Bloch's philosophy of hope and the massive challenge of such secular eschatologies as Marxism), as well as the eschatological teaching of two major documents from the Second Vatican Council (*Lumen gentium* of 1964 and *Gaudium et spes* of 1965), helped to bring about an "eschatological turn" in post-conciliar Catholic theology. This "eschatological turn" not only has meant respect for the all-pervasive eschatological realities in other areas of theology but has also encouraged theologians to write fresh texts on eschatology

as such. It is not exaggerating to say that this sector of theology
has been on the move toward a new identity.

Post-conciliar Catholic eschatologies are often shaped as
follows. They begin with the eschatological preaching of Jesus
himself, which has as its partial background various prophetic,
messianic and apocalyptic themes of the Jewish scriptures, both
those which entered the biblical canon of Catholic Christianity
and those which did not but which reflect, all the same, eschatological beliefs around at the time of Jesus. In announcing and
then dying for the divine kingdom and reign, Jesus revealed
himself as the mediator and fullness of God's future. After
examining the Christological material from the New Testament,
recent eschatologies frequently move to reflect on the eschatological nature of the church. This pilgrim community, which is
or should be totally oriented toward the future and final kingdom
of God, realizes now in anticipation something of that kingdom
and is at its service through its sacramental and pastoral life. As
well as an ecclesiological section, the first part of these post-
conciliar eschatologies often includes reflections on the eschatological nature of our human and Christian existence. In other
words, they offer an anthropology in the key of eschatology.
They then pass to questions about death and what happens there-
after in the life of the world to come: that is, they attempt to deal
in a fresh way with the classical issues of general and individual
eschatology found in the manualist tradition.

As regards the theme of love, however, the post-conciliar
eschatology has practically nothing to say. Let me exemplify
what I mean by mentioning three authors whose work on eschatology has appeared in four or five languages and has been
widely used as texts for courses: Wilhelm Breuning, Joseph
Ratzinger and Christian Schütz. In *Mysterium Salutis* Schütz and
to a somewhat greater extent Breuning do introduce a few
thoughts about the eschatological character of God's love. But in
that work, as in other recent Catholic eschatologies, hope
remains the dominant hermeneutical key. Reflection takes place

in the spirit of *spes quaerens intellectum* (hope seeking understanding).[11]

It was a little surprising to find love playing almost no role
in Ratzinger's eschatology of 1977. In his *Introduction to
Christianity* a brief section echoed Gabriel Marcel by interpret-
ing our resurrection as "the saving deed of the lover who has the
necessary power." There Ratzinger wrote: "Man can no longer
totally perish because he is known and loved by God. All love
wants eternity, and God's love not only wants it but effects it and
is it."[12] It was not that in his excellent 1968 book on the creed
Ratzinger had much to say about love in an eschatological context. But when his work on eschatology appeared in 1977, sur-
prisingly there was even less about love.

Thus far in this essay I have been concerned to do some
preliminary reporting about pre-conciliar and post-conciliar
Catholic eschatology. My aim was largely to establish a prima
facie case that our modern eschatology has hardly been done in
the key of love. In the second half of the essay I want to suggest
what an approach of *amor quaerens intellectum* (love seeking
understanding) might yield for eschatology, above all, in its classical sense of a theological reflection on the last things.

To carry through my experiment of rethinking eschatology
in the key of love, I obviously need to draw attention to some of
the major characteristics of love. At least eight such characteristics should be recalled when we attempt to describe love in the
light of our human and Christian experience.

(1) To begin with, love is creative: it gives life and brings
into existence that which has not yet existed. The procreation
and raising of children offer the classical example of this genera-
tive characteristic of love. But the medical and teaching profes-
sions, the pastoral ministry and the work of artists, writers and
architects also provide rich insights into the life-giving, creative
force of love.

(2) Second, reason alone can never fully account for the
choice and intensity of love. Of course, love is never simply

unmotivated. We can always point to reasons which help to explain the choice of one's marriage partner or one's profession. But by themselves rational motives can never completely explain and justify love and its activity. Being a supremely free act, love is always gratuitous and never compelled. It is a mysterious act of freedom which is creatively self-determining and never coerced or simply controlled by other factors—not even by the force of reason. To be sure, we run up against a real mystery here. How can a loving action be rational and yet not be fully clarified or at least justified by reason? What happens when love leads someone to do things that go beyond the merely reasonable?

There is mystery here in my vision of the interplay of reason and love. Nevertheless, the alternative—love being simply and totally controlled by reason alone—obviously robs love of that spontaneity which we associate with it and which, *inter alia*, is illustrated by the parable of the laborers in the vineyard (Mt 20:1-16). Love is a self-gift which goes beyond reason and the sheerly reasonable.

(3) Love accepts and approves whatever or whomever it loves. It delights in and assents to the beloved being there: "It is good that you exist. I want you to exist." Love's approval entails the firm desire that the beloved should never go out of existence. To say to someone "I love you" is, if I may borrow a classic insight from the French philosopher Gabriel Marcel (1889-1973), to say to that person: "You must not die; you must live forever." Love's profound approval cannot tolerate the idea of the beloved no longer being there.

(4) The redemptive quality of love should be named as its fourth characteristic. In all kinds of situations real love sets people free. It heals the hurts of life. It transforms people and makes their human and Christian growth possible. Love puts smiles on faces, turns the ugly duckling into a beautiful creature and can rescue a life that threatens to go astray. There is truth in the old,

popular wisdom about wild young men needing to be saved by the love of good women.

In a sad, negative way our experience establishes this fourth point. We have all met people who have not been loved or at least feel that they have never been loved by anyone. They can remain hurt, unfree and terribly stunted in their human and Christian lives, unless and until they are profoundly loved and know themselves to be so loved.

(5) Some words of Jesus in John's gospel point us toward a fifth characteristic of love. First, Jesus says: "He who loves me will be loved by my Father, and I will love him and manifest myself to him" (Jn 14:21). Then, a little later in the same final discourse, Jesus adds: "I have called you friends, for all that I have heard from my Father I have made known to you" (Jn 15:15). Love means self-manifestation and self-revelation. I am not referring here to self-indulgent, endless chattering about one's sayings, doings and successes. Real love is different. When it breaks out of itself to reveal its hidden truth, goodness and beauty, it does so with a style that is oriented toward and centered on other persons. We constantly come across and experience the way love opens up in marriage and deep friendship. Friends make known much or even everything to other friends. We manifest ourselves to those whom we love. In an unpretentious manner genuine love is always self-disclosive.

This fifth point closely attaches itself to the fourth, since real self-revelation is always redemptive. Just as Jesus' own loving self-manifestation changed the human situation for all of us, so disclosing oneself in love serves to heal and save others. Not only at the universal level of Jesus himself but also at the individual level of our interpersonal relationships, revelation is redeeming. To adapt St. John, our loving and freely manifested self-truth sets us and others free (see Jn 8:32).

(6) Love reconciles and unites. This sixth characteristic of love is perfectly represented in the parable of the prodigal son, which would be more accurately called the parable of the merci-

ful father (Lk 15:11-32). The love of the father reaches out not
only to welcome home the prodigal but also to cope with the bit-
terness of the elder son.

Of its very nature love is a reciprocal force and remains
incomplete so long as its sentiments are not returned and there is
not a full giving and receiving. Ultimately love is like a hug; you
cannot give one without receiving one yourself. In his second
encyclical, *Dives in misericordia* of 1980, Pope John Paul II
recalled the way love is bilateral and not simply a unilateral act
or process (n. 14). In this century no one has done more to
emphasize the essentially reciprocal nature of love than Maurice
Nédoncelle (1905-1976). For me to love someone necessarily
means to hope that my feelings will be reciprocated. As
Nédoncelle has argued well, this is not a question of selfishly
trying to manipulate or coerce others into loving me. It is a matter of the very nature of love itself as reciprocal.[13]

The full communion of life which love entails does not
mean a smothering union, still less a union that simply absorbs
or reduces one of the parties. Love unites without being destruc-
tive. The greater the loving union, the more personal identity is
safeguarded and selfhood is enhanced. Here the particularly
happy example is, of course, the Blessed Trinity. There the communion of love between the divine persons is supremely perfect;
in no way does this union lessen the distinction of three persons
within one godhead. They live together for each other and in
each other, without disappearing into each other.

(7) The parable of the merciful father ends with those love-
ly words to his eldest son: "It was fitting to make merry and be
glad, for this your brother was dead, and is alive; he was lost,
and is found" (Lk 15:32). Joy inevitably accompanies love and
all those occasions which in a particular way celebrate and
express interpersonal love: a baptism, a bar mitzvah, a wedding,
an ordination, even a funeral. Joy is woven into the very texture
of love. We happily join our special friends or take part in family
reunions. There is no more obvious spinoff from love than joy.

(8) Eight and finally, let me remind you of a theme especially associated with St. Augustine of Hippo (354-430): the connection between beauty and love. Beauty rouses our love; we love what is beautiful.

That theme, made familiar by Augustine's *Confessions* (10.27), leaves us, however, with some important questions. Is the formal object of love not goodness but beauty? Can something be truly good without also being beautiful, or truly beautiful without also being good? St. Thomas Aquinas (ca. 1225-1274) did not explicitly include beauty in his list of transcendentals—that is, concepts which apply to all being. Nevertheless, he did argue that goodness and beauty, if logically distinguishable, coincide in fact. His position encourages us to keep endorsing Augustine's conviction about our loving what is beautiful.[14]

In the last few pages I have been sketching eight points suggested by our human and Christian experience of love. Obviously these eight points do not cover all that could be said. An adequate analysis of love would range much more widely. Nevertheless, can this analysis help to put a pattern on what we believe God will do for us at the end? What does it look like if, point for point, we apply this analysis of love to eschatology?

(1) First, God showed infinite divine love by creating the universe and its center, human beings. God's overflowing goodness gave birth and gives birth to everything that is. All created reality is the fruit and expression of the divine love.

If God's love is the key to the creation and conservation of the world, all the more should it be seen as the key to the new creation of all things at the end. Divine love lay behind the original creation when God gave life to what had not yet existed. A fortiori will that love lie behind the new creation when God will give new, transformed and definitive life to what once existed but has died.

(2) One can assign some reasons for God's original act of creation. Yet more than an edge of mystery remains when we attempt to answer the question: Why did God create? It was and

is a mysterious act of divine freedom to create and from moment to moment sustain in existence all the things that have been created. A fortiori we cannot account in a merely rational way for the mystery of God's love that promises us resurrected life with the new heaven and the new earth. Reason alone cannot explain the love already shown in creation and the even greater love that will be shown in the mystery of the new creation's consummation.

(3) According to the priestly account of creation, God saw the goodness of everything that was made—above all, the goodness of human beings made in the divine image and likeness (Gen 1:27). In and through love God deeply approved of us and our world. God delighted in creation and, in effect, said to each and all of us: "It is good that you exist. I want you to exist."

The loving approval of God brings with it even more. It offers something that human love alone can never achieve: life forever. The divine love is more powerful than death (Song 8:6-7).[15] It will not only deliver us from death but will also hold out to us a new, transformed and definitive life to come.

(4) Fourth, from the Old Testament on, love has proved a classic theme for expressing God's redeeming activity on our behalf. God's love sets us free from the forces of evil; it heals us and transforms us. All agree that redemption will reach its consummation in the world to come. That is equivalent to saying that the activity of God's redeeming love will reach its climax at the eschaton.

(5) As we have already seen, revelation and redemption are two sides of the same coin. God's self-revelation is essentially redemptive; and, vice versa, redemption through the divine love must be known, in order to be effective or at least fully effective.

The letter to Titus catches beautifully the deep relationship between revelation and salvation when it declares, "The grace of God has appeared for the salvation of all human beings" (Tit 2:11). A few verses later the same letter expresses this same thought but in a way which attends more explicitly to the role of love in the divine self-revelation that has already occurred: "When the goodness and loving kindness of God our Savior appeared, he saved us" (Tit 3:4-5). Love has prompted the divine self-manifestation, a self-manifestation in Christ that has saved us.

Like other books of the New Testament, the letter to Titus associates revelation even more with the future, with what it calls "the appearing of the glory of our great God and Savior, Jesus Christ" (Tit 2:13). At the end no one will have to look hard to find God. Through the divine love we have already been made children of God. When Christ comes again, through the divine love both redemption and revelation will be consummated. As 1 John states, "It does not yet appear what we shall be, but we know that when he appears we shall be like him, for we shall see him as he is" (1 Jn 3:2). The divine love which has already initiated the process of salvific self-disclosure will definitively complete its work at the end.

(6) Love's reciprocity will be perfected when Jesus comes again. That will be the final homecoming, the welcome home which never ends. I used earlier the parable of the merciful father to illustrate the reconciling, reciprocal nature of love. I may be excused if I use the parable in an extended sense and speak of heaven as our finally coming home from a "far country." In the fourth gospel, Jesus himself puts it this way: "When I go and prepare a place for you, I will come again and will take you to myself, that where I am you also may be" (Jn 14:3).

This final, mutual, loving union with God through Christ will not destroy our individuality. God will be "all in all" (1 Cor 15:28), but not in the sense of swallowing us up into the deity. On the contrary, our personal identity with its bodily history will be safeguarded and our true selfhood enhanced. At the end love will mean the highest possible union but not our disappearance back into the divine source from which we came.

(7) The boundless joy that God's love holds out to/for us at the eschaton gets expressed by the New Testament through two

characteristic images: a marriage and a banquet (which may in fact be a marriage banquet). Jesus pictures the coming kingdom as a final feast: "Many will come from east and west and sit at table with Abraham, Isaac and Jacob in the kingdom of heaven" (Mt 8:11). His parable of the watchful slaves contains the amazing reversal of roles: when he returns, their master himself will serve them at a late-night feast (Lk 12:35-38). The book of Revelation portrays our heavenly home, the new Jerusalem, as a beautiful bride coming to meet her spouse, the Lamb of God (Rev 21:2-5, 9). Those who "are invited to the marriage feast of the Lamb" can only rejoice and be glad (Rev 19:9). Both now and even more at the end, love brings with it real joy.

To express the utterly joyful change Christ has brought us and will bring us, the New Testament uses the language not only of spousal relationship, but also of friendship (e.g. Jn 15:15) and filiation (e.g. Rom 8:29; Gal 3:26; 4:5-7). Love and the joy of love run like a golden thread through all three kinds of relationships.

(8) At present the divine beauty of the risen Lord stirs our love, even though it remains mysterious—visible only indirectly through sacramental and human signs. His beauty is hidden, to be glimpsed really but not too directly unless we are gifted with special mystical graces. In the world to come we shall see God as God is and live face to face with the divine beauty. Contemplating the infinite beauty of God, we will freely but inevitably love God and others in God. The divine beauty will see to it that we finally and completely fulfill the commandment to love the Lord our God with all our heart and our neighbor as ourselves (see Mk 12:30-31).

Such then is the substance of my vision of "love seeking eschatological understanding"—that is, love seeking to understand and interpret the *eschata* or last things. To be sure, the vision is incomplete but it has decisive advantages. It is obviously incomplete, and that in two ways. First, much work remains to be done in spelling out what this vision of love would say about such particular eschatological issues as the individual's death, purgatory and bodily resurrection. Second, my vision is incomplete because nowadays it is at our peril that we bypass the questions arising at the interface between science and theology.

If we take seriously the discoveries and dominant theories of contemporary cosmology, our universe, which started with a big bang around fifteen billion years ago, is going to end badly—either by collapsing back on itself into a cosmic melting pot (the big crunch) or through continued expansion into final decay. The scientific problem presents itself like that at the level of the whole universe. As regards our planet earth, current ecological degradation, which may be already irreversible, rightly raises great alarm about the biological future of the human race. Our species appeared no more than 150,000 years ago: first as *homo sapiens neantherthalensis* and then as *homo sapiens sapiens*. How much longer do we have? Both cosmic and planetary forces threaten us. Is science putting an important question here about our Christian doctrine of the end of the world?

Alongside the challenges and daunting questions coming from developments in physics, cosmology and other sciences, there are also findings that can readily fuel our wonder at God's creation. We now know that, traveling at the speed of light, it would take us 100,000 years to go from one side of our galaxy, the Milky Way, to the other. There are 3,000 million other galaxies in the known universe, as far as light and time will let us see. Facts like these stretch and stagger the mind. But my point here is not so much to enter into details. It is simply to note how material reality has been found to be vast, intricate and amazing in its evolution and to argue that theologians, and in particular those who specialize in eschatology, would be acting foolishly if they were to ignore the extraordinary developments in current cosmology—from Edwin Hubble (1889-1955) to date. They would also be unwise to ignore the impact that current cosmology has made on popular attitudes not only about the origin and the destiny of the universe but also on our ways of looking at ourselves within the universe. Theologians need to be concerned with the cosmic, with material creation, and not restrict themselves to the spheres of the personal and the historical.

Do I strain credibility here by suggesting that love just might provide the answer to the grand unified theory or GUT, the holy grail for which many contemporary scientists search? After all, love is the essence of God (see 1 Jn 4:8,16). Through God, love can surely be expected to be the most fundamental characteristic of all created reality. Perhaps we can find our grand unified theory or GUT through love, the most intimate bond of all things.[16] If we do, we would not be so very far from Dante's vision of the love which "moves the sun and the other stars."

Obviously, this proposal needs to be elaborated extensively and nuanced very much before it could even win a hearing from most scientists. Here I simply wish to suggest the idea as a possible path to pursue, while recognizing how it may be a violent attempt to relate two different fields (natural science and theology) with their quite different languages.

Beyond question, my vision of "love seeking eschatological understanding" is incomplete. On the one hand, it should be brought to bear on the important, specific issues in eschatology. On the other hand, it needs to confront in detail the challenges coming from modern science.

But this vision, I would argue, has its marked advantages. It goes beyond the human standpoint which characterizes both pre-conciliar and post-conciliar eschatology and which gets expressed in the slogan "hope seeking understanding" (*spes quaerens intellectum*). God's love belongs to a higher order of things. Hopefully it is not ultimate arrogance to attempt to ponder through the eyes of divine love what God has in store for us. I have drawn my analysis of love largely from human and Christian experience. But I have also applied that analysis to what God will do at the end in the consummation of human life and our world.

Here, as elsewhere, St. Paul is an encouraging and enlightening guide. The apostle's references to human beings loving God (Rom 8:28; 1 Cor 2:9; 8:3; Eph 6:24; perhaps Rom 5:5) are few and far between when compared with his references to the divine love for us (e.g. Rom 5:8; 8:37, 39; 9:25; 2 Cor 9:7; Gal 2:20; Eph 1:4; 2:4; 5:2, 25; 1 Thess 1:4; 2 Thess 2:13, 16).

The Holy Spirit is the eschatological gift, so the New Testament assures us. The Spirit is the divine love poured into our hearts (Rom 5:5), working in the world and guiding history toward the end, which will be the fulfillment of God's redemptive gift of love. The final coming of Christ will be nothing more and nothing less than the definitive coming of divine love. In other words, the eschaton is best seen as the climactic love event for the whole human family, the event through which God promises to become an immediate, personal presence for us in Jesus Christ.[17]

Notes

1. Irenaeus, *Adversus haereses,* 4.14.1.

2. In Christianity the theme of love as a path, or even *the* path, to knowledge is as old as John's gospel. Let me quote just one voice, that of Evagrius Ponticus (346-399), who in his *Capita practica ad Anatolium* calls love "the door of knowledge" (PG 40. 1221).

3. In his *Anastasis* (London: Wiley and Putnam, 1845) Bush wrote of "the great scheme of scriptural eschatology, or the doctrine of the last things" (p. v), "the great scheme of eschatology" (p. ix), "scriptural eschatology" (p. 275), "prophetic eschatology" (p. 300), "scriptural eschatology" (p. 348) and "the general scheme of eschatology" (p. 365).

4. This was Volume 12 in his *Systema locorum theologicorum;* see RGG (1957) 1. 1587.

5. In *The Christian Faith* (Edinburgh: T. & T. Clark, 1928; German original 1830) Schleiermacher used "eschatology" and

"eschatological" when presenting "the last things" (pp. 703, 710). Writing on "Eschatologie" in *Lexikon der katholischen Dogmatik,* ed. W. Beinert (Freiburg i. Breisgau: Herder, 1987), Josef Finkenzeller remarked: "The word 'eschatology' achieves greater significance through F. Schleiermacher, such that it enters common theological usage" (p. 141). He might have added that Schleiermacher's own eschatological thinking has been commonly found deficient, by both Protestant and Catholic theologians.

6. L. Ott, *Fundamentals of Catholic Dogma* (St Louis: B. Herder, 1958), pp. 476, 478, 484. The German original was published in 1952.

7. M. Bordoni and N. Ciola, *Gesu nostra speranza: Saggio di escatologia* (Bologna: Edizioni Dehoniane di Bologna, 1990); G. Greshake and G. Lohfink, *Naherwartung, Auferstehung, Unsterblichkeit: Untersuchungen zur christlichen Eschatologie* (Quaestiones Disputatae 71; Freiburg: Herder, 1982); Z. Hayes, *Visions of a Future: A Study of Christian Eschatology* (Wilmington: Michael Glazier, 1989); M. Kehl, *Eschatologie* (Würzburg: Echter, 1986); G. O'Collins, *Man and His New Hopes* (New York: Herder and Herder, 1969); K. Rahner, *Foundations of Christian Faith* (New York: Seabury, 1978), pp. 431-447; idem, "Eschatology," *Sacramentum Mundi,* vol. 2 (New York: Herder and Herder, 1968), pp. 242-246; J. Ratzinger, *Eschatology* (Washington: Catholic University of America Press, 1989); J.L. Ruiz de la Peña, *La otra dimension: escatologia Cristiana,* 3rd ed. (Santander: Sal Terrae, 1986).

8. *Theological Investigations,* vol. 4 (Baltimore: Helicon, 1966), pp. 323-46.

9. This trend, already encouraged by the biblical work of Johannes Weiss (1863-1914) and Albert Schweitzer (1875-1965), really set in when the second edition of Karl Barth's *Römerbrief* appeared in 1922 (English tr. *The Epistle to the Romans;* London: Oxford University Press, 1968).

10. J. Moltmann, *Theology of Hope* (New York: Harper and Row, 1967). The German original was published in 1964.

11. "Allgemeine Grundlegung der Eschatologie," *Mysterium Salutis,* vol. 5 (Zurich-Einsiedeln-Cologne: Benziger, 1976), pp. 553-692; "Systematische Entfaltung der eschatologischen Aussage," ibid., pp. 779-890. Hope is also the hermeneutical key to the recent document from the International Theological Commission, "De quibusdam quaestionibus actualibus circa eschatologiam," *Gregorianum* 73 (1992): 395-435, which at least sixteen times refers to "hope" (*spes*) in its introduction (pp. 396-401). (For an English translation cf. International Theological Commission, "Some Current Questions in Eschatology," *Irish Theological Quarterly* 58 [1992]: 209-243.)

12. *Introduction to Christianity* (New York: Herder and Herder, 1970), p. 271; see also pp. 274, 275. The German original was published in 1968.

13. M. Nédoncelle, *La réciprocité des consciences* (Paris: Aubier, 1942).

14. For details see P. Sherry, *Spirit and Beauty* (Oxford: Clarendon Press, 1992), pp. 43-45.

15. See the use made of the Song of Songs by Pope John Paul II in *Dives in misericordia,* n. 8.

16. Here I obviously approach Teilhard de Chardin's thinking about the role of love-energy, the basic, immanent force which unifies, personalizes and "totalizes" all things as they are drawn, after cosmogenesis, biogenesis and noogenesis, through Christogenesis to the source and object of agape in the Omega Point, the cosmic Christ. For some details see my *Jesus Risen* (Mahwah: Paulist Press, 1987), p. 192.

17. For some helpful criticisms of this paper, I wish to thank three colleagues at the Gregorian University: Fr. Luis Ladaria, Fr. Vittorio Marcozzi and Fr. Willibrord Welten. I am deeply grateful to them, but I do not in any way want to make them responsible for what I have written.

Eschatological Events Accompanying the Death of Jesus, Especially the Raising of the Holy Ones from Their Tombs (Matt 27:51-53)

RAYMOND E. BROWN, S.S.

In the biblical narratives of the passion of Jesus, there is no more eschatological, nay even apocalyptic, passage than Matt 27:51-53 where at the death of Jesus the veil of the sanctuary is rent from top to bottom, the earth is shaken, the rocks rent, the tombs opened, and the bodies of the fallen-asleep holy ones raised. This is a neglected passage, and to many an embarrassing one; and so a paper devoted to it has its own challenge.[1]

Moreover, at this particular time this passage is a most appropriate topic for still another reason. We are within a few months of the fiftieth anniversary of the issuance of Pope Pius XII's encyclical "Divino afflante spiritu," the magna carta of modern Catholic biblical studies, on September 30, 1943. One of the primary principles inculcated by that encyclical was the diversity of literary genre within the Scriptures, liberating us from the fallacy that had dominated our outlook for many years, namely, that all biblical narrative is history. I hope in this paper to show that the wealth of this Matthean passage can be tapped only when we recognize that it is not history (and never was

intended as such) but the dramatization of an apocalyptic understanding of the death of the Lord as marking the end of times—a
dramatization in quasi-poetic format illustrating the way that
theology was understood in popular circles in the late 1st
Christian century.

To facilitate a comparison of passages, I offer below a very
literal translation of the reactions to Jesus' death as described in
the Synoptic Gospels and in the *Gospel of Peter*,[2] an early 2nd-
century popular account of the passion that combines folkloric
imagination and memories of the canonical Gospels (probably
gained by its author from hearing them read publicly, and perhaps from having read one or the other in times past).[3]

In the Synoptic Gospels there are two types of reactions to
Jesus' death, first, physical reactions of an extraordinary nature,
and then the reactions by those people who were present and
who had seen the physical reactions. These people include the
centurion, those who kept watch over Jesus, the assembled
crowds, those known to Jesus, and the Galilean women. In providing this translation I am interested primarily in the physical
reactions (which in the canonical Gospels are set off in bold
face), and so I do not include a complete account of the reactions by people.

Translation

Mark 15:33-39: **³³And the sixth hour having come, darkness came over the whole earth until the ninth hour.** ³⁴And at the ninth hour Jesus screamed with a loud cry, "*Elōi, Elōi, lama sabachthani?*", which is interpreted, "My God, my God, for what reason have you forsaken me?" ³⁵And some of the bystanders, having heard, were saying, "Look, he is crying to Elijah." ³⁶But someone, running, having filled a sponge with vinegary wine, having put it on a reed, was giving him to drink, saying, "Leave (be). Let us see if Elijah comes to take him down." ³⁷But Jesus, having let go a loud cry, expired.

³⁸And the veil of the sanctuary was rent into two from top to bottom.

³⁹But the centurion who had been standing there opposite him, having seen that he thus expired, said, "Truly this man was God's Son."

Matt 27:45-54: **⁴⁵But from the sixth hour darkness came over all the earth until the ninth hour.** ⁴⁶But about the ninth hour Jesus screamed out with a loud cry, saying, "*Ēli, Ēli, lema sabachthani?*"—that is, "My God, my God, to what purpose have you forsaken me?" ⁴⁷But some of those standing there, having heard, were saying that "This fellow is crying to Elijah." ⁴⁸And immediately one of them, running and taking a sponge full of vinegary wine and having put it on a reed, was giving him to drink. ⁴⁹But the rest said, "Leave (be). Let us see if Elijah comes saving him." ⁵⁰But Jesus, again having shouted with a loud cry, let go the spirit.

⁵¹And behold, the veil of the sanctuary was rent from top to bottom into two. And the earth was shaken, and the rocks were rent, ⁵²and the tombs were opened, and many bodies of the fallen-asleep holy ones were raised. ⁵³And having come out from the tombs after his raising they entered into the holy city; and they were made visible to many.

⁵⁴But the centurion and those who with him were keeping (guard over) Jesus, having seen the (earth) shaking and these happenings, feared exceedingly, saying, "Truly this was God's Son."

Luke 23:36: Moreover, also the soldiers mocked, coming forward, bringing forward to him vinegary wine....

23:44-47: **⁴⁴And it was already about the sixth hour, and darkness came over the whole earth until the ninth hour, ⁴⁵the sun having been eclipsed. The veil of the sanctuary was rent in the middle.** ⁴⁶Having cried out with a loud cry, Jesus said, "Father, into your hands I place my spirit." But having said this, he expired.

⁴⁷But the centurion, having seen this happening, was glorifying God, saying, "Certainly this man was just."

GPet 5:15-6:22: ⁵:¹⁵But it was midday, and darkness held fast all Judea; and they were distressed and anxious lest the sun had set, since he still was living. [For] it is written for them: "Let not the sun set on one put to death." ¹⁶And someone of them said, "Give him to drink gall with vinegary wine." And having made a mixture, they gave to drink. ¹⁷And they fulfilled all things and completed the(ir) sins on their own head. ¹⁸But many went around with lamps, thinking that it was night, and they fell. ¹⁹And the Lord screamed out, saying, "My power, O power, you have forsaken me." And having said this, he was taken up.

²⁰And at the same hour [midday] the veil of the Jerusalem sanctuary was torn into two. ⁶:²¹And then they drew out the nails from the hands of the Lord and placed him on the earth; and all the earth was shaken, and a great fear came about. ²²Then the sun shone, and it was found to be the ninth hour....

10:41-42: (Those present at Sunday dawn were hearing a voice from the heavens addressed to the gigantic figure of the Lord who has been led forth from the sepulcher): ⁴¹"Have you made proclamation to the fallen-asleep?" [42]And an obeisance was heard from the cross, "Yes."

Extraordinary Physical Reactions to Jesus' Death in Mark and Luke

Mark. Our oldest preserved Gospel has divided the physical reactions temporally: darkness over the whole earth before Jesus died (in reaction to the immediately preceding mockery of Jesus by the passers-by, the Jewish authorities, and the co-crucified), and the rending of the sanctuary veil after Jesus died (in reaction to the way in which even his plaintive protest to God was mocked, leaving him to die rejected totally by those around him). Both darkness and the rending of the veil are wrought by God as signs of judgment.[4]

As for darkness, one of the exodus plagues was the darkness "over all the land" for three days called down by Moses as a punishment for the Egyptians (Exod 10:21-23). Perhaps the best OT parallel to the Gospel portrayal, however, may be found in the darkness that marks "the day of the Lord," conceived of as a day of judgment and punishment: "a day of wrath...a day of darkness and gloom" (Zeph 1:15). Joel 3:4 (RSV 2:31) predicts, "The sun will be turned to darkness...at the coming of the great and terrible day of the Lord." Amos 8:9-10 seems particularly pertinent, even if the vocabulary differs from Mark's: "And on that day, says the Lord God, the sun shall set at midday, and the light shall be darkened on earth in the daytime.... I will make them mourn as for an only son and bring their day to a bitter end." Against this background one can interpret Mark to mean that, while the mockers demanded of Jesus on the cross a sign (i.e., that he come down from the cross), God is giving them a sign foretold by the prophets as part of a judgment on the world and a warning of punishment that was now beginning. For Mark the rending of the veil of the sanctuary means that God has abandoned the building that was God's house; it is no longer a sanctuary; and indeed in the future, perhaps already in Mark's time, it will cease to exist.

The Jews present who were mocking Jesus on the cross were not chastened by the darkness, but the Roman centurion is moved by the combined signs that colored how Jesus had died. He becomes the first human being in Mark to confess the truth about Jesus, "Truly this man was God's Son." Those who insist on sheer history have had to ask how the centurion, standing at the knoll of Golgotha north of the city walls, could have seen the rending of the veil of a sanctuary that faced east—the latest historicizing solution has been to move the site of the crucifixion to the Mount of Olives on the east and to assume that the outer veil of the sanctuary, visible from that mount, was meant. The historicizers have also had to ask where the centurion got his theological training to perceive and phrase the divinity of Jesus in a way that anticipated Christian post-resurrectional preaching. In face of that difficulty, the solutions proposed often reduced his perspicacity by having him confess Jesus only as "a son of God," i.e., a noble human being.

All such reflections are inappropriate. "Divino afflante spiritu" strongly emphasized the literal sense of the Scriptures, i.e., the meaning the writer was trying to make comprehensible to his audience. Probably Mark's hearers/readers (possibly in Rome), and perhaps even the evangelist himself, would not have known the geography of Jerusalem, or the precise directional relationship between the site of Golgotha and the Temple sanctuary, or how many veils the sanctuary had and which one was involved.[5] Neither the Gospel audience nor Mark would have reflected on what precise theological comprehension was possible for a pagan soldier on a Friday afternoon in Jerusalem some thirty or forty years in the past. "Son of God" in the centurion's confession was the divine title that Mark and his audience used in their own liturgical practice in the 60s or 70s to confess Jesus, and they would have understood this man to be the first one to come to Christian faith. Unpleasantly polemical as it may be, they would have understood the scene as Christians have ever since: Those who professed belief in the one to whom Jesus had just prayed as "My God" mocked Jesus; yet a Gentile without such background saw in the extraordinary darkness and the rending of the veil of the Jewish sanctuary God's vindication of Jesus and God's judgment on the scoffers.[6]

During the Sanhedrin trial in Mark, Jesus had been mocked as a false prophet because of a claim that he would destroy the sanctuary and because he affirmed his identity as the Messiah, the Son of the Blessed. On the cross he had been mocked on the same two issues: let him come down from the cross if he was the one who would destroy the sanctuary and if he was the Messiah. But the moment he died, God acted to fulfill both those prophetic stances: the veil of the sanctuary was rent, and Jesus' identity as truly God's Son was acknowledged. Jesus' public ministry began (Mark 1:10-11) when the heavens were "rent," so that the voice of God could speak from there and declare of Jesus, "You are my beloved Son" (1:10-11). Now, by inclusion, the public ministry has ended as God from heaven intervenes again, rending the veil of the sanctuary and bringing the centurion to confess, "Truly this man was God's Son!" The work of evangelizing has begun: what God confessed in heaven is now confessed by human beings on earth.

Luke. While Mark surrounds the death of Jesus with the two signs of darkness and the rending of the veil, one before and one after the death, Luke has moved the rending of the veil before the death and joined it to the darkness. This is not because Luke has better historical knowledge but because of the "order" that he professed he would introduce into the story of Jesus (Luke 1:3: a more "orderly account"). If he kept the rending of the veil after the death, that negative sign would be mixed with three positive reactions by people. Such a mixture of negative and positive reactions would disturb orderliness. By moving the rending of the veil, Luke has achieved the nigh perfect paral-

lelism illustrated in the accompanying chart. Luke has removed
the rending of the veil to before the death and yoked it with the
darkness so that now the two negative signs are together. Since
the rending of the sanctuary veil occurs before the death of
Jesus, it is less immediately the effect of the death of Jesus.[7]
Stressing the positive in his theology, Luke has preferred to con-
centrate on the salvific reactions to the death of Jesus among a
symbolically wide range of people (thus anticipating the spread
of the Gospel): a Gentile, the Jewish populace, and Jesus' followers.[8]

Luke 23:26-28	Luke 23:47-49
Three positive reactions by people before Jesus is put on the cross	Three positive reactions by people after Jesus dies on the cross
An individual, Simon of Cyrene, brings the cross behind Jesus	An individual, the centurion, confesses Jesus' true identity
A large multitude of people follow Jesus, beating themselves	The crowds return (home), striking their breasts
The daughters of Jerusalem follow Jesus, lamenting for him	The women from Galilee see these things

Yet, if to some extent Luke has de-eschatologized Mark's
portrayal of the physical reactions connected with Jesus' death,
Luke has added eschatology and another dimension in harmony
with his own theology by appending the phrase "the sun having
been eclipsed" (23:45a) as an explanation for the darkness. Once
more this has offered extraordinary difficulty for those who have
interpreted the narrative simply as history, for there cannot be an
eclipse in the period of the full moon, and Jesus died at Passover
which was celebrated at the full moon of the month of Nisan.

This problem was already seen by Origen[9] who hinted that
the idea of an eclipse was introduced by anti-Christians to dis-
credit the Gospels. Ingenious solutions have been proposed.
Some have favored a less troublesome translation of *tou hēliou*

eklipontos: not "the sun having been eclipsed" but the blandly meaningless "the sun having failed." Ancient copyists obligingly produced a less troublesome Greek reading: *kai eskotisthē ho hēlios,* "and the sun was darkened/obscured," and modern interpreters who have accepted that reading suggest that a dust storm came up to produce such a darkness. A moon eclipse rather than a solar eclipse has been brought into the picture by those who appeal to Peter's sermon in Acts 2:20 where he quotes from Joel to the effect that "the sun shall be turned into darkness, and the moon into blood." Other scholars, contending that Luke did refer to an eclipse of the sun, argue that God interrupted the laws of nature at the death of Jesus by producing an eclipse when ordinarily none was possible. Strangely, however, no ancient astronomer took note of what should have been one of the more amazing phenomena of all time, especially since the eclipse lasted over the whole earth for three hours, and the maximum length of an attested solar eclipse has been seven minutes and forty seconds. Still others argue that we should translate "over all the land," not "over the whole earth," and thus confine the phenomenon to Judea where it may not have been noted by an astronomer.

More detailed reflection on these various suggestions, not all of which can be easily dismissed, may be found in my commentary. Here I note solely that I find far more plausible the interpretation that Luke did mean to refer to an eclipse of the sun, perhaps not knowing about the full-moon problem[10] but surely recognizing that the three-hours-over-the-whole-earth description was hyperbole. He may have been thinking about a solar eclipse that took place in the Near East within a few years of Jesus' death (a death that most likely took place at Passover in April of A.D. 30 or 33). Evidence points to a solar eclipse, lasting 1 1/2 minutes, that occurred in parts of Greece, Asia Minor, and Syria on November 24, A.D. 29. There are possible pertinent references to it in ancient authors, but the date they assign varies. Concerning an eclipse that happened in the reign of Tiberius (A.D. 14-37), Origen (*Contra Celsum* 2.33) reports that Phlegon[11] made a record of it along with an earthquake.[12] Eusebius in his *Chronicle* for the 18th-19th year of the reign of Tiberius[13] reports that Phlegon says that in the 4th year of the 202nd Olympiad there was a great eclipse of the sun, outdoing all that preceded. It became like night at midday. The specified year would have run from July 1, A.D. 32 to June 30, A.D. 33.[14] Writing some one hundred years after the event, Phlegon may have fixed on the wrong year for the eclipse of A.D. 29. Writing some fifty years after the event, Luke may have connected a vague memory of the solar eclipse of November A.D. 29 with Jesus' death which actually took place in April a year or several years later.

Why would Luke be interested in such a reference? In the Lucan infancy narrative the advent of Jesus was hailed as "a rising light [*anatolē*] from on high, appearing to those who sat in darkness and the shadow of death" (1:78-79). But now is the period of Jesus' death; and the Lucan Jesus, as he was being arrested, exclaimed that this was "the hour" of his enemies "and the power of darkness" (22:53). Luke would have assumed that this eclipse was controlled by God who employed one of the eschatological signs of the last times mentioned in the OT to signal the death of the Son. This mindset is apparent in Acts 2:17-21 when on Pentecost Peter cites from Joel 3:1-5 (RSV 2:28-32) signs (including darkening of the sun) showing that what happened to Jesus marks "the last days."

There may have been another dimension to Luke's communication, however, that goes beyond such OT background and beyond the eschatological motifs. A noted eclipse bringing darkness at noon before the death of Jesus may have served to underline the impact of that death upon the Roman Empire (which, like "the ends of the earth" in Acts 1:8, is what Luke would have meant by "the whole earth" in 23:44). In providing a setting for Jesus' birth Luke 2:1 connects it with the edict "from Caesar Augustus that a census should be taken of the whole

world—the first census when Quirinius was governor of Syria."
Now, in fact, there never was a census of the whole Roman
world under Caesar Augustus; but a local Roman census of
Judea, well-remembered by Jews because it produced a revolt,
did take place when Quirinius was governor of Syria. Yet that
was at least ten years after the most probable date of Jesus' birth
and did not affect Galilee or Nazareth, as Luke would imply.[15]
Luke mentioned a census in relation to the birth of Jesus because
he wanted to show that this birth was an event of global importance that involved even the Roman emperor and the Roman
governor, and he has a parallel interest at Jesus' death. In each
case the evangelist, who was not a research historian, would
have drawn on memories of famous events which he could not
date precisely but which occurred in the general period of Jesus'
birth and death, in order to center Jesus in the world scene.

We can see the importance of such a cosmopolitan
approach when we consider how Luke's readers in the
Hellenistic world with little background in OT "day of the Lord"
imagery might have understood the darkness, eclipse, and rending of the sanctuary veil described in 23:44-45. There is abundant Greco-Roman evidence that extraordinary signs were commonly thought to accompany the death of great or semidivine
men. If we confine ourselves to authors who wrote within 100
years before or after Jesus' death, we find that Plutarch
(*Romulus* 27.6) reports that at the demise or departure of
Romulus "the light of the sun was eclipsed."[16] When Julius
Caesar was put to death, Plutarch (*Caesar* 69.4) speaks of an
obscuring of the sun; and Josephus (*Ant.* 14.12.3; #309)
describes it as an occasion on which "the sun turned away."[17]
Indeed, Pliny (*Natural History* 2.30; #97) mentions this death to
exemplify a wider principle: "Portentous and long eclipses of
the sun, such as when Caesar the dictator was murdered." Luke
adapted the extraordinary phenomena surrounding Jesus' death
(which he took over from Mark) to form an inclusion with extraordinary events surrounding Jesus' birth; in both instances he

attached worldwide significance to them in order to appeal to the interests of his readers. This theological restructuring prepares us to understand a similar effort by Matthew.

Extraordinary Physical Reactions to Jesus' Death in Matthew

Like Mark, Matthew divides the physical phenomena by placing the three-hour darkness before the death of Jesus and the rending of the sanctuary veil after the death. However, he has complemented that rending by a much longer list of extraordinary phenomena in the aftermath of the death. In order to study the Matthean passage carefully, it is helpful to set up the verses in a line-by-line structure:

> 51a: And behold, the veil of the sanctuary was rent from
> top to bottom into two.
> b: *And the earth was shaken,*
> c: *and the rocks were rent;*
> 52a: *and the tombs were opened,*
> b: *and many bodies of the fallen-asleep holy ones were raised.*
> 53a: And having come out from the tombs
> b: after his raising
> c: they entered into the holy city;
> d: and they were made visible to many.

I shall comment first on the origins of this material which Matthew did not find in Mark and then on the use that Matthew makes of it.

In the passion narrative Matt has a considerable amount of vivid material absent from Mark. In my commentary, *The Death of the Messiah,* I contend that although there are elements of Matthean style in these stories, and therefore the evangelist has rewritten and reshaped them, there are enough peculiar elements to indicate that Matthew did not create them. Rather, he drew on a collection of popular stories that fleshed out the passion of Jesus by imaginative reflection—the same type of popular material that he drew upon in the infancy narrative with its account of the magi from the East, the star that came to rest over Bethlehem, the wicked king Herod and the chief priests and the scribes, the slaughter of the male children, and the flight into Egypt.[18]

Thus far in the passion narrative this popular material would include: (a) *the episode of Judas' hanging himself* (27:3-10) with its thirty pieces of silver, the insensitivity of the chief priests and the elders who are scrupulous about blood money but care nothing for the guilt involved in giving over an innocent man to death, and the "Field of Blood" remembered to Matthew's day; (b) *the incident of Pilate's wife's dream* (27:19) whereby she knows that Jesus is a just man; (c) t*he description of Pilate washing his hands* (27:24-25) of the blood of an innocent man, while all the people say, "His blood on us and on our children." If we count the phenomena we are discussing as (d), yet to come after the burial of Jesus is (e) *the story of the guard placed at the sepulcher* (27:62-66; 28:2-4,11-15). There the chief priest, the Pharisees, and the elders will be shown as unprincipled scoundrels who conspire with Pilate to block the resurrection. Their plans will be foiled by an earthquake and an angel who descends from heaven to open the tomb. They will offer pieces of silver to purchase the lie that the disciples of Jesus came and stole the body,[19] a false tradition that has circulated among the Jews to Matthew's own day. These incidents or stories peculiar to Matthew's passion narrative are marked by vivid imagery (blood, dreams), by extraordinary heavenly phenomena (earthquake, dead rising), and, alas, by great hostility toward Jewish authorities, sometimes accompanied by a sympathetic presentation of Gentiles—characteristics of Matt's infancy material as well.

Many of these same features appear in Matthew's account

of the phenomena that greeted the death of Jesus: shaking of the earth, the opening of tombs, the raising of many bodies of the fallen-asleep holy ones (27:51b-53). A factor that increases the likelihood of a popular origin is the semi-poetic format of the material. In setting off this material above, I italicized four clauses (51bc, 52ab) so that readers could see both their similarity to each other (four coordinated simple sentences or main clauses, beginning with *kai*, in which the verb is an aorist passive) and their differences from the more complicated v. 51a (which Matt took over from Mark) and from v. 53.[20] It is almost as if the basic aorist passive pattern of 51a, indicating divine action, constitutes a small poetic quatrain consisting of two couplets (51b and c are interrelated, as are 52a and b) with the earthquake of 51bc leading into the results described in 52ab. V. 53 has the appearance of a drawn out reflection on the events of 52ab.[21] Poetic refrains are often a part of the popular presentation of an event, and are attested in NT references to the aftermath of the death of Jesus.[22]

A close poetic parallel is found in *On the Pasch* of Melito of Sardis, composed *ca.* A.D. 170. In the context of describing the Lord's death and the darkness that accompanied it, Melito (98; SC 123.118) writes four couplets in which, while the first lines decry the insensitivity of the Jews, the second lines describe the corresponding terrestrial or celestial phenomena thus:

The earth was trembling...
The heavens feared[23] ...
The angel rent his clothes[24] ...
The Lord thundered from heaven,
and the Most High gave a cry.

Notice that the contextual reference to darkness is followed by allusions to an earthquake and a loud cry. Similarly and contemporaneously, *The Ascents of James* (Pseudo-Clementines 1.41.3.) reports that the whole world suffered with Jesus: the sun was darkened; the stars were disturbed; the sea was roiled up;

the mountains were moved; the graves were opened; and the veil of the Temple was rent as if lamenting the destruction hanging over the place.[25]

I suggest that this exercise of poetic imagination employing apocalyptic imagery is the way many Christians gave expression to the eschatological value of the death of Jesus. The endtime was at hand, and these were the signs of divine judgment. If for Christians the death of Jesus was the catastrophe that called forth divine intervention, for the Judaism contemporary with Matthew the crucial moment was the destruction of the second Temple by the Romans. Josephus, the Jewish historian, knew perfectly well that Roman soldiers physically did this action, but that did not stop him from attributing it to God's righteous anger over divisions and impieties among the Jews. In *War* 6.5.3; #288-309 he tells of some eight wonders that occurred between A.D. 60-70 and served as ominous, God-given portents of the coming desolation of the Jerusalem Temple by the Romans, even though many of the Jews foolishly took them as positive signs. (In recounting these portents, I italicize motifs that may be compared to the phenomena in Matt.) In the *heavens* there were a sword-shaped star; a *comet* that continued for a year; and at 3 A.M. a light as bright as day shining around the altar and the sanctuary; chariots and *armies seen throughout the country in the clouds* before sunset (told with special emphasis that this is not a fable). In the *Temple* area there were many signs: a cow giving birth to a lamb; the massive brass eastern *gate of the inner court opening* by itself at midnight, even though scarcely movable by twenty men; *at Pentecost* the priests in the inner court hearing a *collective voice, "We are departing from here"* (i.e., the sanctuary[26]); years of woes against Jerusalem and sanctuary uttered by Jesus bar Ananias whom the Jerusalem authorities seized, beat, and handed over to the Romans to be put to death, only to have him released by the governor as mad. Tacitus, who would have been in Rome during the last years of Josephus' life there and probably depends on

him, lists (*Hist.* 5.13) many of these same phenomena in reference to Titus' destruction of the Jerusalem Temple.[27]

Very early the relationship between the extraordinary signs
at Jesus' death and extraordinary signs at the destruction of
Jerusalem and the Temple was seen. St. Jerome, in a half-dozen
passages written between A.D. 380 and 409, associates with the
rending of the sanctuary veil the shattering of the Temple lintel
at the time of the Roman destruction, the departure of angelic
guardians, and the desertion of the house of the Lord. Indeed, he
even claims that in an apocryphal gospel written in Hebrew let-
ters, "We read not that the veil of the Temple was rent, but that
the Temple lintel of great size was heaved over."[28] Clearly the
Jewish tradition about the portentous phenomena surrounding
the destruction of the Temple (in this case phrased by Josephus)
has colored the understanding of the phenomena accompanying
the death of Jesus. Both sets of actions express God's wrath, and
those of A.D. 30/33 foreshadow the greater destruction in 70;
indeed, the line between the two is blurred. The rending of the
sanctuary veil which functioned on a symbolic level ultimately
becomes the physical shaking or upheaval of the Temple lintel,
as occurred in the destruction of the building by the Romans. A
catalyst in connecting the Christian presentations of 30/33 and
70 is OT prophecy referring to events in the Temple; indeed,
some of Jerome's pertinent passages are an interpretation of
Isaiah. With this background of OT prophecy, apocalyptic signs,
and a context of God's judgment, let us now comment briefly on
the individual incidents reported by Matthew.

Earth Shaken (27:51b). In Matt alone a star greeted the
birth of "the King of the Jews" (2:2,9); and so it is not surprising
by way of inclusion that at the death, besides darkness coming
over all the earth (27:45), the earth itself would shake. Above
we saw that both Origen and Eusebius, in describing the eclipse
recounted by Phlegon, made reference to a severe earthquake.
Probably Matt's reference to a shaking of the earth contributed
to the shift in later Christian tradition (just reported from

Jerome) from the rending of the sanctuary veil at Jesus' death to a fracturing and overturn of the Temple lintel.

There are numerous OT examples of shaking the earth as a sign of divine judgment or of the last times.[29] In the context of God's blazing wrath being manifested toward the people of God who are so evil, Jer 4:23-24 reports: "I looked at the earth and it was waste and void; at the heavens and their light was gone; I looked at the mountains and they quaked, and all the hills were moved." The combination of darkness and earthquake as part of judgment is found too in the description of the day of the Lord in Joel 2:10: "Before them the earth shall tremble and the heavens shake; the sun and moon shall be darkened, and the stars shall withdraw their light." In Jesus' warnings during the ministry (Matt 24:7-8; Mark 13:8), earthquakes mark the beginning of the travails of the last times. Thus, Matt's readers, if they were familiar with any of this background, should have had little difficulty recognizing in the shaking of the earth that accompanied the rending of the sanctuary veil an apocalyptic sign of God's judgment evoked by the cruel death to which the Son of God was made subject. As for readers with primarily a Greco-Roman background, Virgil reported that, besides the "veiling of the sun" (n. 17 above), the Alps quaked at the murder of Caesar. Indeed, when Lucian wants to burlesque the death of a famous man, he mentions an earthquake as a sign that greeted his departure (*De morte Peregrini* 39).

Rocks Rent (27:52a). This might be considered an example of poetic parallelism, using other words to say the same thing as "the earth was shaken." Nevertheless, often the power of God in smashing the solid rocks is a special item in describing judgment.[30] In 1 Kings 19:11-12 as part of what might be expected in a theophany, we hear of a strong wind splitting the mountains and crushing the rocks, and after that an earthquake. Zech 14:4 describes the final judgment with God coming to stand on the Mount of Olives and "rending" it into two halves; Nahum 1:5-6 reports that when the wrath of God is let loose, the mountains are shaken and the rocks are smashed asunder. In *Testament of Levi* 4:1, a poetic passage with a format not unlike that of Matt 27:51b-52b, as God effects judgment on human beings, "the rocks are rent, and the sun darkened."

Tombs Opened (27:52a). For Matt, God's action of opening the bowels of the earth after the death of Jesus is an inclusion with God's opening the heavens in the beginning of the ministry at the baptism of Jesus (3:16).[31] The connection of the tomb opening with the preceding rending of the rocks is splendidly visible in the Dura Europos synagogue where wall-paintings portrayed the raising of the dead as part of the enlivening of the dry bones in Ezek 37—a 3rd-century A.D. tableau[32] that is very helpful in understanding how Matthew and/or his readers might imagine the scene he is narrating. There in the splitting of a mountain covered by trees (almost surely the Mount of Olives rent by an earthquake[33]), rocks are rent, thus opening up tombs burrowed into the sides of the mountain and exposing bodies of the dead and their parts. A figure is depicted who may be the Davidic Messiah (see Ezek 37:24-25) bringing about this raising of the dead.

Earlier and contemporary with the writing of Matt there is testimony to the importance that Ezek 37 had for the just who died for their convictions about God. At Masada where Jewish Zealots made their last stand against the Roman armies in A.D. 73, in the floor of the synagogue were found fragments of a scroll on which was written Ezekiel's account of his vision of the raising of the dead bones. Consequently, even apart from the Dura-Europos portrayal, Ezek 37:12-13 may be the key passage behind Matt's description both in this line and in what follows, for it offers the only *opening* of tombs (as distinct from the simple raising of the dead) described in the OT: The people of God are assured that they will come to know the Lord because: "I will open your tombs, and I will bring you up out of your tombs, and I will lead you into the land of Israel." Previously, each description of an individual phenomenon in Matt's list of four in

27:51b-52b, while partially repeating in poetic parallelism what preceded (the shaking of the earth rent the rocks and thus opened the tombs), also provided a new vista. That is true here as well, for the sign has now moved from the heavens (darkness) and the earth (rent sanctuary veil, shaken earth, rent rocks) to under the earth. Which tombs were opened? The answer to that is involved with the identity of the "holy ones" in the fourth phenomenon.

Many Fallen-asleep Holy Ones Raised (27:52b). "Asleep" is a frequent NT euphemism for the dead.[34] In the context of judgment *I Enoch* 91:10 envisions that "the just shall arise from their sleep" (also *IV Ezra* 7:32); and *II (Syriac) Baruch* 21:24 regards Abraham, Isaac, and Jacob as asleep in the earth. In Matt's description the "holy ones" must be Jews who died after a saintly life, those whom Matt elsewhere (13:17; 23:29) associates with prophets of old under the title "the just [*dikaioi*]." The *Testament of Levi* 18:10-11 foresees that the anointed high priest of the last days "will open the gates of Paradise...and will give to the holy ones to eat from the tree of life." Hitherto the apocalyptic signs have been negative (darkness, rent sanctuary veil, earthquake), but this sign shows the positive side of the divine judgment centered on the death of God's Son: the good are rewarded, as well as the evil punished.

Jews who believed in bodily resurrection would have expected that all the holy ones (just) should have been raised and received the kingdom (Dan 7:22; Luke 14:14), or even that all human beings should have been raised and been assigned different fates by God (Dan 12:2; John 5:28-29). A selective raising as here is very peculiar and has led to speculation: What tombs were opened and which holy ones were raised? The Matthean context (27:53-54) in which the opening of the tombs is part of the phenomena visible to the centurion and other guards on Golgotha and in which those raised become visible in the holy city indicates that Matt is thinking of tombs of holy ones in the Jerusalem area close to where Jesus died.

Although some commentators have proposed that Matt is describing the deliverance of the great known figures of OT history whose reward has been delayed until the redemption brought by Jesus,[35] relatively few of them (Adam, David) were supposed to be buried in the Jerusalem area. Appeal has been made to Matt 23:37 which charges that Jerusalem killed the prophets, suggesting the possibility of their having been buried there. Other commentators have thought of holy ones closer to Jesus' time or involved with him, even if there is only legend about their burial place. In antiquity John the Baptist was nominated as one of the raised bodies, although that was queried by later commentators (Cornelius a Lapide) on the grounds that several churches (Rome, Amiens) claimed to have relics of his preserved head. The *Gospel of Nicodemus* (*Acts of Pilate*) 17:1 says that Jesus raised Simeon, the aged man who took the baby Jesus into his arms (Luke 2:25-28), as well as Simeon's two sons who had died recently. Indeed their tombs could still be seen opened, and these risen worthies were alive and dwelling in Arimathea!

All such speculation is unnecessary, for this popular, poetic description is deliberately vague—its forte is atmosphere, not details. Note that the features of fear, lack of recognition, doubt, and demanded proof that accompany the resurrection and appearances of Jesus are *not* found in Matt 27:52-53. The identity of the risen Jesus as the same one whose crucifixion and death had been witnessed was important for NT writers; but here the awesome power of God's action, not the identity of the raised, is the issue. The coming of the kingdom of God in the ministry of Jesus was understood not as the final manifestation of the kingdom (i.e., the culmination when the Son of Man would gather before him all the nations, assigning those who are to inherit the kingdom prepared for them from the foundation of the world, as in 25:31-34) but as an inbreaking inaugurating and anticipating it. Similarly this raising of "many bodies" as Jesus dies is not the universal final resurrection but an inbreaking of

God's power signifying that the last times have begun and the judgment has been inaugurated. At the Sanhedrin trial Jesus warned the high priest and the authorities judging him, "From now on you will see the Son of Man sitting at the right of the Power and coming on the clouds of heaven" (26:64). The darkness, the rent sanctuary veil, the shaken earth, the rent rocks, the opened tombs, and the raised bodies of the holy ones are the apocalyptic trappings that illustrate the partial fulfillment of the divine judgment implied in that prophetic warning, as the All-Powerful God responds to the death of the Son of God.

When one appreciates the symbolic, poetic, and popular apocalyptic character of the four lines of 27:51b-52b with the phenomena they describe, they offer no major problem. They are clearly attached to the death of Jesus on Friday afternoon (only v. 53 shifts the focus to Easter), whence the ominous judgmental tone that precedes the raising of the holy ones. But the situation has been complicated by Christian theological attempts to understand chronologically the various aspects of Jesus' death and going to his Father. One attempt fills in the interstice between death on Friday and discovery of the empty tomb early Sunday by having Jesus descend into hell; but while that idea is found elsewhere in the NT, it is not in mind here. (It is found in the more developed phenomena represented by *GPet* 10:41-42 where, as the Lord is led forth from the sepulcher, a voice from heaven speaks, "Have you made proclamation to the fallen-asleep?", and from the cross there is an obedient response, "Yes.") Another attempt, which we must discuss in relation to the next verse in Matt, makes all victory flow from the resurrection of Jesus.

Coming out of the Tombs, Entry into the Holy City, and Appearances (27:53). I have already noted that the style of writing changes noticeably when we pass from the short coordinated lines of the quatrain (27:51b-52b), phrased in the aorist passive, to the complex participial, active phrasing (much closer to Matt's normal style) in 27:53. The moment that is the focus of

theological interest also changes. Is not Jesus "the first fruits of
the fallen-asleep" (1 Cor 15:20), "the first-born from the dead"
(Col 1:18)? Does not the oldest preserved Christian writing on
the subject (1 Thess 4:14) give the proper order: "Jesus died and
rose; so through Jesus God will lead out with him those asleep"?
How, then, can the many bodies of the fallen-asleep holy ones
have been raised (Matt 27:52b) before Jesus himself was raised?
We cannot enter here into all the vagaries of proposed transla-
tions of Matt 27:53, but a number of scholars attribute all the
action of v. 53 to the Easter period after Jesus' resurrection.
However, I prefer to understand it thus: "And having come out
from their tombs [on Friday], after Jesus' resurrection [Sunday]
they entered into the holy city; and they...." Jesus' death made
possible not only the raising of the holy ones but their emer-
gence from the tombs; Jesus' resurrection made possible the
entry of the raised holy ones into the holy city and their appearances there.

What does Matthew envision by reporting that the bodies
of the fallen-asleep holy ones, once raised, entered "the holy
city"? The use of that designation for Jerusalem in passages such
as Isa 48:2; 52:1; Rev 11:2, as well as earlier in Matt (4:5-6),
rules out all other terrestrial candidates.[36] Nevertheless, many
interpreters balk at the thought of many known risen dead being
seen in Jerusalem—such a large-scale phenomenon should have
left some traces in Jewish and/or secular history! Consequently,
they appeal to the use of "holy city" for a new, heavenly
Jerusalem in Rev 21:2,10; 22:19 ("the city that is to come" of
Heb 13:14), and interpret Matt 27:53c to mean that the risen
dead entered heaven after Jesus' resurrection. Yet there is a fatal
flaw in this heavenly "holy city" interpretation of Matt 27:53c:
"they were made visible to many" in 53d can scarcely apply to
heaven! Given that appearances in earthly Jerusalem are surely
intended, some early Christian thinkers contended that these
holy ones had not been raised to eternal life, but (like those
raised by Jesus during his ministry) they were only resuscitated

to ordinary life. A miracle was performed but not the miracle of a resurrection like that of Jesus. They were "made visible" in their ordinary bodies, and they would die again.

This conception lies behind the already mentioned claim in the *Gospel of Nicodemus* that those raised included Simeon and his two sons who had died recently (and thus presumably had not corrupted). The ordinary character of their renewed existence is confirmed by the report that they were living at Arimathea. Eusebius (EH 4.3.2) quotes from the apologist Quadratus who lived during Hadrian's reign (117-138) concerning those who had risen from the dead: "After Jesus' departure they existed for a considerable time, and certain of them have reached even our own days." While this folklore partially resonates with the popular character of the vivid phenomena associated with the death of Jesus,[37] it is quite foreign to the apocalyptic thrust of those phenomena. If we remember that the criterion of interpretation must be what Matthew intended by his narrative (not what we think happened), the concatenation of signs in the heavens, on the earth, and under the earth scarcely allows us to think that the culmination was a resuscitation to ordinary life. Those who were resuscitated by Jesus during his ministry did not have to appear or to be made visible to some; that description makes sense only of those who are raised to another sphere, even as Jesus was raised and appeared.

Overall, then, the following seems the best interpretation of 27:53: To vv. 51b-52b, a poetic piece describing four eschatological phenomena associated with Jesus' death, Matt had added two other interrelated eschatological phenomena associated with Jesus' resurrection, namely, emerging from the tombs to enter Jerusalem and being made visible to many. Thus, those who were raised to eternal life at the death of Jesus made their appearances after his resurrection. These holy ones entered Jerusalem, the holy city near which God will judge all at the end of time; and their appearances both attested that Jesus had conquered death and promised that eventually all the holy ones

would be raised. Matthew does not report what happened to
them after the Jerusalem appearances any more than he reports
what happened to Jesus after his last appearance (28:16-20).
Presumably it was self-evident that both he and they, having
been delivered from death, dwell henceforth with God.

I have argued that the quatrain in Matt 27:51b-52b, composed from interwoven echoes of Scripture, was taken over by
Matt from popular circles that gave full rein to symbols in inter-
preting Jesus' death as an eschatological event anticipating the
final times and God's judgment on the world. By adding the
quatrain to what he received from Mark (51a: rending of the
sanctuary veil), Matthew now had a set of extraordinary happenings (earth shaken, rocks rent, tombs opened, bodies raised) at
the end of the Gospel to match the extraordinary happenings at
the beginning (star symbolizing the Messiah rising and coming
to rest over Bethlehem, Gentile magi adoring Jesus, Herod
killing the children). To that quatrain Matthew himself added v.
53 (a verse noticeably closer to Matthew's own style) to extend
the eschatological symbolism to Easter and connect it to Jesus'
own resurrection.

Matt would have been acting under the influence of a
strain of Christian thought that characterized Jesus as the first-
born or first fruits of the dead—an aspect seemingly neglected
by localizing the raising of the fallen-asleep holy ones on Friday
before Jesus' resurrection. Without changing that localization,
Matt has done more justice to the priority of Jesus by having the
holy ones who had been raised on Friday enter the holy city and
be made visible only "after his raising [= the raising of him])."

The freedom of early Christians to attach eschatological
symbolism to any one of the events in the sequence death-resur-
rection-ascension-gift of the spirit (which from God's viewpoint
are only different aspects of one timeless moment) is illustrated
further in Acts 2:16-20. That passage sees fulfilled at Pentecost
what was prophesied by Joel: before the coming of the day of
the Lord, wonders in heaven above and signs on earth below

(blood, fire, a cloud of smoke, sun turned to darkness, moon turned to blood). The Acts passage is the Lucan equivalent of Matt 27:51b-53 in emphasizing apocalyptic signs.

Matthew's addition also enhanced the fulfillment of Scripture. We have seen how much Ezek 37 with its creative description of the enlivening of the dry bones influenced Jewish imagination in picturing the resurrection of the dead. The first part of Ezek 37:12-13, "I will open your tombs," probably shaped the third line of the quatrain of Matt 27:51b-52b, "And the tombs were opened." But the Ezek passage continues: "And I will bring you up out of your tombs, and I will lead you into the land of Israel. Then you shall know that I am the Lord." Even as elsewhere Matthew enhances the scriptural background and flavoring of material taken from Mark, so here scripturally he goes beyond the quatrain by offering in 27:53 the fulfillment of the rest of the Ezek passage: "And having come out from the tombs,...they entered into the holy city [of Jerusalem]." These holy ones are Jews; in the next verse Matthew will present Gentiles (27:54: the centurion and the guards who were with him) and their confession of faith. From Jesus' birth (which involved Joseph and the magi) to his death, Matthew is interested in showing that Jesus brought salvation to both Jew and Gentile alike. Thus, in Ezekiel's language, through God's Son they come to "know that I am the Lord."

Notes

1. The passage under discussion here is treated in detail in volume 2, §43 of my commentary, *The Death of the Messiah* (New York: Doubleday, 1994), along with §42 on the eclipse in Luke. There I shall give the technical scholarly support for the positions that I advance here and a complete bibliography. I prefer to stress intelligibility in this necessarily brief paper.

2. Henceforth *GPet*. Other abbreviations to be used here include: Mark/Matt for passages or structures where Matt fol-

lows Mark so closely that they may be treated as one witness. Matt will be used for the Gospel, and Matthew for the evangelist.

3. In "The *Gospel of Peter* and Canonical Gospel Priority" (*New Testament Studies*) 33 [1987]: 321-343) and in my commentary I have argued in detail against the contention of J. D. Crossan (*The Cross That Spoke: The Origins of the Passion Narrative* [San Francisco: Harper & Row, 1988]) that *GPet* represents the oldest written passion narrative. Unfortunately, he has made that thesis, which has little following, a major pillar in his reconstruction of *The Historical Jesus* (San Francisco: HarperCollins, 1991), a construction that in many places borders on fiction.

4. The passive "was rent" makes God the agent. There have been many attempts, which I reject in my commentary, to make the rending of the veil a positive sign. Jesus' passing through the veil in Heb 10:19-20 is a positive sign, but the liturgical setting of the Day of Atonement in Hebrews is absent here.

5. Despite the enormous amount of research dedicated to the outer/inner veil issue and to the esoteric symbolism of the respective veil, I reject the value of the whole enterprise in relation to the Gospel description. Mark (7:3-5) had to explain to his readers elementary Jewish purity customs. Can we seriously think he expected them to interpret the rending of the veil against an unsupplied background of the curtain arrangements in the Herodian edifice and of the way they were colored?

6. In *Testament of Levi* 10:3, when God can no longer endure Jerusalem because of the wickedness of the priests, the veil of the Temple is rent so that their shame can no longer be covered.

7. Writing in the post-70 period, Luke knows that the Temple has been destroyed; but that destruction most vividly affected a generation later than those who stood at the place of crucifixion —that is why, in his warning to the daughters of Jerusalem about the inevitability of divine punishment, Jesus

told them to weep for themselves *and their children*. Because there is an element of ignorance among those who put Jesus to death (Luke 23:34; Acts 3:17), a period of grace is granted before it will become Christian truth that God does not dwell in a house made by hands, and that Jesus of Nazareth has destroyed this holy place (Acts 7:48-49; 6:13-14). And before the destruction comes in the time of the children, the Temple will continue to serve. When Jesus ascends to heaven on Easter Sunday evening, the disciples will return to the Temple to praise God (24:53). Peter and John will go into the Temple precincts (Acts 3:3), and the apostles will be in the Temple every day (5:42). Even Paul will go to the Temple to fulfill a vow (21:26). In Luke's mind it was not only because the authorities rejected Jesus in his lifetime but also because they rejected the miracles and preaching of his apostles that God ultimately caused the Temple to be destroyed.

8. Luke alone combines with the women from Galilee some male acquaintances of Jesus. In the commentary I shall argue that these are not the Twelve (or Eleven) but unnamed disciples, similar to Luke's mention of the seventy(-two) disciples during the ministry. Thus Luke has both men and women followers of Jesus looking on from a distance. He cannot break the conventional picture that they did nothing to assist Jesus, but at least they did not flee.

9. *Commentariorum Series* 134; *In Matt.* 27:45 (GCS 38.271-274).

10. S. Killermann ("Die Finsternis beim Tode Jesu," TG 23 [1941]: 165-166) points out that Albert the Great who had scientific abilities may not have known that Passover occurred at the full moon.

11. Phlegon, a Greek from SW Asia Minor, was a historian who lived in the reign of Hadrian, A.D. 117-135. Origen places the reference "in the 13th or 14th book, I think, of Phlegon's Chronicles [*Olympiades*]."

12. Yet in commenting on Matthew (n. 9 above), Origen is

careful to point out that Phlegon did not say that the eclipse took place at the full moon.

13. GCS [2d ed.] 47.174-175. Tiberius reigned from 14 to 37—was Eusebius thinking of A.D. 31-32? U. Holzmeister ("Die Finsternis beim Tode Jesu," *Biblica* 22 [1941]: pp. 404-411) raises the issue of a possible confusion between a moon eclipse on April 3, A.D. 33 and the sun eclipse on November 24, A.D. 29.

14. Some would use this evidence to argue for the death of Jesus in April 33, but such reasoning does not remove the impossibility of a solar eclipse at Passover.

15. We know from Acts 5:33-37 that Luke was confused about the date of that census because he places it after the uprising of Theudas, which took place decades later.

16. Similarly Ovid (*Fasti* 2.493) uses the expression "the sun fled," and Cicero (*De re publica* 6.22): "the sun...appeared to be extinguished."

17. Ovid (*Metamorphoses* 15.785) describes "the sad face of the sun," and Virgil (*Georgics* 1.467): the sun "veiled its shining head."

18. I use the term "popular" to cover a transmission of Jesus material other than by the preaching, kerygmatic transmission that marked much of the Synoptic material or by the marshaling of synagogue-trial evidence that shaped the Johannine material. I intend nothing pejorative historically, theologically, or intellectually in the designation. Indeed, in the popular stories detectable in Matt perceptive theological issues are being raised, and the quality of the language is often quite pungent.

19. The episode of Judas and the silver followed Matt 27:1 when "all the chief priests and elders of the people took a decision [*symboulion lambanein*] against Jesus that they should put him to death." In Matt's guard-at-the-sepulcher story (28:11-12) the chief priests gather with the elders and, "having taken a decision," give silver to the soldiers.

20. While v. 51a also has an aorist passive, the basic action is

modified by a long descriptive phrase. V. 53 begins with a participial construction plus a phrase, and the first principal verb is active not passive.

21. I have deliberately not punctuated 53abc to illustrate the problem of whether 53b should be read with 53a or 53c.

22. 1 Pet 3:18-19, consisting of five or six poetic lines, has an eschatological tone: the one who died in the flesh and was made alive in the spirit goes and preaches to the spirits in prison. Eph 4:8, consisting of three lines, portrays Christ ascending on high, leading a host of captives. Perhaps the NT analog closest in form to Matt 27:51b-52b is 1 Tim 3:16, composed of six lines (short main clauses) in a pattern of three couplets: Christ is the unnamed subject and all the verbs are in the aorist passive. Frequently this poem is interpreted as ranging from the incarnation to the ascension, but the whole could refer to the death of Jesus and its aftermath.

23. Probably a reference to the darkness that covered all the earth.

24. This refers to the rending of the sanctuary veil. Tertullian (*Adv. Marcion* 4.42.5; CC 1.660): "The veil of the Temple was rent by the breaking forth of an angel leaving the Daughter of Zion."

25. It is not clear whether this is derivative from Matt or from an independent variant tradition of signs accompanying the death of Jesus.

26. The presence of an angel or angels (spirit or spirits) in the Holy of Holies is assumed. Sometimes these may be the angels who adore the divine presence (as in Isa 6:2-3) or who guard the sanctuary; other times, like the angel of the Lord, they may represent an anthropomorphic description of God.

27. Tacitus says that there were ill-omened signs that the Jews foolishly looked on as favorable. They included: armies fighting in the heavens; fire lighting up the Temple; doors of the Holy Place abruptly opening; a superhuman voice declaring that

the gods were leaving it and at the same time a great movement of those departing.

28. Epistle 120 (*Ad Hedybiam* 8; CSEL 55.489-90). This Gospel was actually in Aramaic and used by the Nazoreans of the Berea or Aleppo region. For the other references, see *The Death of the Messiah.*

29. E.g., Judg 5:4; Isa 5:25; 13:9-13; 24:18; Ezek 38:19; Joel 4:15-16 [RSV 3:15-16]; Hag 2:6,21.

30. The phrase "the rending of the rocks" occurs in the LXX of Isa 2:19 in the description of where those who flee the day of the Lord will hide their idols.

31. By contrast Mark 1:10 and 15:38 make the inclusion between the *rending* of the heavens and of the sanctuary veil.

32. The Dura synagogue was built *ca.* A.D. 200. The paintings, including the Ezekiel painting on the north wall, stem from the period following the enlargement in A.D. 244. The literature on the painting is abundant, e.g., H. Riesenfeld, *The Resurrection in Ezekiel xxxvii and the Dura-Europos Paintings* (Uppsala: Lundequistska Bokhandeln, 1948); R. Wischnitzer-Bernstein, "The Conception of the Resurrection in the Ezekiel Panel of the Dura Synagogue," JBL 60 (1941): 43-55.

33. See Zech 14:4 where God comes to exercise judgment on the Mount of Olives. Matt's insistence in the next verse (27:53) that they entered the holy city (of Jerusalem) may have been influenced by Zechariah's locale for the judgment.

34. 1 Thess 4:13; 1 Cor 15:20; John 11:11; 2 Pet 3:4.

35. Heb 11:39-40, after going through the exploits of many great OT figures, says, "And all these, though proved by faith, did not receive the promise...so that apart from us they should not be made perfect." Ignatius (*Magnesians* 9:2) writes of the OT prophets: "When the one arrived for whom they were rightly waiting, he raised them from the dead." See more specifically *Martyrdom (Ascension) of Isaiah* 9:17-18.

36. Why does Matt use the designation "the holy [*hagios*] city" rather than speaking directly of Jerusalem? Is he playing

on an established designation that contains the same word he has just used for "holy ones" (*hagioi*) in 52b?

37. Previously I have cited parallels in Greco-Roman descriptions of the death of famous people or institutions to show that the Gospel phenomena would be intelligible to readers from that background, no matter what theological value they might assign to such portents. Cassius Dio (*History* 51.17.5) reports that at the fall of Alexandria to the Romans, "the disembodied spirits [*eidōlon*] of the dead were made visible."

Contributors

Raymond E. Brown, S.S., is Auburn Distinguished Professor Emeritus of Biblical Studies at Union Theological Seminary, New York.

Blase J. Cupich is the Rector of the Pontifical College Josephinum, Columbus, Ohio.

John P. Galvin is Associate Professor of Systematic Theology at The Catholic University of America, Washington, D.C.

Walter Kasper is the Bishop of Rottenburg-Stuttgart.

Gerald O'Collins, S.J., is Professor of Fundamental Theology at the Pontifical Gregorian University, Rome.

T-27
*39f